Hide and Seek

Zara Jamieson

Hide and Seek

Printed in the United States of America

For permissions, inquiries or requests to book author for events, please send correspondence to: zjhideandseek@gmail.com

Print ISBN: 978-1-7322623-0-0
E-Book ISBN: 978-1-7322623-2-4

Dedicated To...

My Daughters...

You two beautiful gems inspire me daily to keep pushing forward. I love you with all my heart, and I will spend my days trying to be a better version of myself for you. My prayer for you both is to be strong kingdom women. Always look to the hills from whence all your help cometh!

My Mommy...

Thank you for loving me, guiding me, praying for me and always believing in me. Our time was shortened, but the memories that we share are for a lifetime. Alzheimer's cannot take away our love, bond, time and laughs. I am grateful that you are still alive, and I believe that in your own special way, you are very much aware of my challenges and triumphs. "Lady in Red," I love you something fierce! Always and forever.

My Sisters...

For every tear, frustrating moment, heartache, stress, time of uncontrollable laughter, prayer session, real talk session and disagreement, I thank you. Our sisterhood is strong; we love hard and pray harder. Thank you for being anchors for me and my girls during trying times!

PJ...

You pushed the chapter "Hide" out of me when I wanted to stop. You sent me back to the playground to stand up to my bully! I am beyond grateful that you did. Thank you!

My Love...

I permissioned God for you, and He answered. Restoration at its best! So refreshing. I love you, Jay.

Contents

Hide and Seek

The process of unpacking one's personal storms and tragedies amongst strangers feels scary and uncomfortable. My story is a *complicated* one. It has always seemed complicated to me personally because I have lived in the midst of it, experiencing every moment. I've always simply accepted it as "my story." However, when I think about it, the truth is, this story is really not "mine" at all. It's for everyone.

You see, God allowed these things to happen to me intentionally… for a purpose. They happened solely for His glory and according to His will so that one day, my experiences could be used to help others! Thus, with an obedient spirit, I will do my best to unpack this story, becoming completely naked and vulnerable with my testimony.

Author's Note

This memoir is a work of creative nonfiction. I have attempted to recreate events, locales and conversations based on my memory of them and have made every effort to ensure that the accounts provided are accurate. While characters, incidents and dialogues are real, I have altered identifying characteristics such as individual names, physical properties, occupations, and places of residence in order to protect the privacy and maintain the anonymity of the people involved.

one

The Beginning

I was eight years old when my mother, second oldest brother and I moved to California from New York. I was in the third grade, living in a new state, going to a new school, and looking for new friends. This was where I had my first encounter with Justin, the boy who would eventually become my husband later in life. Of course, we were only young, innocent friends in primary school at the time; we had no idea that we would be reintroduced to each other as adults, and many years later, fall in love and get married.

After elementary school, we each went on to live our separate lives without giving the other a second thought. However, as fate would have it, one day, our lives intersected once again. I vividly remember the evening when he and I ran across each other's path. It was a Thursday night in December of 2003, and it was very close to Christmas, if I remember correctly. My best friend and I were just exiting a store when I saw him.

In a low voice, I asked, “Is that Justin?”

She nodded her head and said, “That sure is.”

I began to smile. He was very attractive.

Still walking, I mumbled in a low tone, “If he doesn’t say anything, keep walking.”

“Okay,” she responded in the same low tone. We both laughed and continued to head to our car, where he was standing.

Justin made sure that his eyes connected with mine and said, “Bree Hill!” He flashed the sexiest smile at me.

We all stopped and started to make small talk. My bestie clearly picked up on the instant attraction between Justin and me. After exchanging a few words, she told him it was good to see him again, and then she headed to the car to give us a minute to talk by ourselves.

Justin complimented me on how I had turned into a beautiful woman, and I, in turn, acknowledged that he too was very attractive.

He asked, “Would it be okay if we exchanged numbers and kept in touch?”

Without hesitation, I replied, “Yes.” I gave him my number.

Justin and I spoke with one another briefly over the next couple of weeks. Then, in January, I received a random phone call from him on a Friday evening, just as I was getting out of my hair stylist’s chair.

“Hey, what are you doing tonight?” he asked.

I answered, “Nothing really special. Probably hanging with one of my girlfriends. Why, what’s up?”

Justin said that he was having an impromptu 30th birthday party at a local lounge. “I would love for you to come,” he said.

"Really? Well, I shouldn't feel special, because I am just hearing of this party the same night."

"Actually, you should, because you are the only one that I personally called and invited myself," he explained.

I smiled and said, "Okay. Well, you just might see me there."

Justin responded, "I really hope so, B," and hung up.

My girlfriend Mo and I got dressed and went to the party. I have to admit the party was jumping! Within the first 15 minutes of us arriving, Justin came over. He was dressed to a T, smelling good and looking good. He came over to me and gave me the biggest hug ever.

"I am so happy you made it!" he said. I told him I was happy to be a part of his birthday celebration. I thanked him again for the personal invite and expressed that I really appreciated it.

I noticed that another woman was standing nearby on Justin's right-hand side. She kept looking in my direction while he and I were talking. I guess we were talking too long without a proper introduction. She tapped him and said "Hey, baby," as she stared directly at me.

I smiled, looked Justin in his eyes, and said to the woman, "Hi, I'm Bree," with my hand extended.

She gave me the fakest smile and said, "I am Alexis, his *girlfriend*."

The look on Justin's face was priceless. It was a look of embarrassment, confusion and irritation. He quickly stated in a monotone voice, "This is my girl, Alexis."

I smiled and nodded my head. "It's really nice to meet you." I looked back at my girlfriend Mo, who was also standing next to us, and smiled. "Mo, are you ready to get a drink?" I asked.

Mo, who had caught on to what was happening, said with a sarcastic laugh, “Yes! A drink is necessary at this moment!” I excused us and we headed to the bar, busting up with laughter.

As we walked away, I looked back at Justin, and he was doing exactly what I’d expected: he was watching us walk away with a “deer caught in the headlights” look.

Mo and I stayed and continued to have a good time. After all, the party was jumping, the music was good, and she and I knew more people at the lounge than just Justin.

A little while later, Justin came over – without his girlfriend – and asked, “Is it okay if I have a few moments to speak with you alone?”

“What do you want?” I asked in an unfriendly tone.

“I’m sorry about that.”

“Sorry about what? Your girlfriend? Why would you be sorry for her?”

“She and I are in the midst of breaking up,” he said. He went on to say that he didn't think she would be coming to his party.

Before I could even respond, Justin got the same familiar tap on his shoulder again. This time, his girlfriend made sure that I was able to hear her loudly and clearly.

“Every time I look around, you are either talking to this female or you’re around her. What’s the deal with you and her?” she asked accusingly.

I walked away and didn’t even acknowledge her anger; I wasn’t giving her that satisfaction.

Writing on the Wall

As I was walking away, I heard Justin yell at her in a rage. I couldn't make out exactly what he was saying, but it definitely sounded out of character for the charming, mild-mannered person that I thought that he was. I didn't realize it then, but in retrospect, I realize that this was writing on the wall, something that I should have paid particularly close attention to when it happened.

At 6 a.m. the next morning, my phone rang. I reluctantly answered without looking at the caller's name on the screen.

"Hello?" I said sleepily.

"Good morning, B," the voice on the other end answered in the tone of a whisper. It was a very deep and sexy voice.

I immediately became alert as I recognized the voice. "Really!" I responded in the most disgusted tone that I could muster up that early in the morning.

"Before you say another word," he said, "I am sincerely sorry for what happened last night. You are such a classy lady and you handled that situation flawlessly. She and I are truly in the process of breaking up. I just don't want to hurt her because in the past, she's had my back. But I'm no longer happy in the relationship. She's aware of that, but she doesn't want it to end. Then, I ran into you, and I am definitely interested in getting to know you seriously. All I'm asking you, if I may, is some time to tie up some loose strings so that I can fully give you and us the attention that is needed. Do you think that is possible?"

"I'm not a home wrecker," I answered, "so whatever you have to do should be based on what you want to do regardless of whether you and I end up getting to know each other intimately." Then, I asked, "How long are you asking me for? I'm just curious."

Justin chuckled, in such a way that implied, "Got her!" He answered, "Give me a couple of weeks to tie everything up. But I hope to still be able to keep in contact with you. I want to hear that sweet, sexy voice as much as possible."

"That may be a possibility. Let's play it by ear. No promises," I said.

"Okay. No promises," he echoed.

Two weeks passed by quickly, and Justin did exactly what he said he would do: he moved out of his girlfriend's place and broke up with her completely. Because he was so timely about handling his business and ending the unhappy relationship, I attached the word "trustworthy" to my perception of his character. It seemed to be the truth of who he was, based on his actions. At least, that is what I thought.

At the time that I began my new relationship with Justin, I'd already had a daughter, Sierra. I gave birth to her when I was 21 years old. She is the love of my life, and no words can truly express the depth of love that I have for her.

Now, at the age of 29, I was a young single mother working and living with my parents. My daughter's father, Nigel, and I had a relatively good friendship. At this point in our lives, our relationship was over. However, our common denominator was our love for the beautiful child that we were blessed with, so we worked together as a team to co-parent her and provide her with all of the love and support we could.

During this season of my life, Justin and I had entered into a full-blown relationship. In retrospect, I realize that this was my first mistake. Justin had come out and expressed his feelings to me first, and he pursued me without any distractions or remnants of feelings for other women. Because of this, I gave myself permission to fall in love with him; I promptly gave him my heart.

Justin was a father, himself. He'd already had three children from two prior relationships: a daughter from one relationship, and a son and daughter from another relationship. Needless to say, because of our instant relationship that led us to blend our lives with one another, we also blended our children in the same manner, without talking it through. This was mistake number two.

The reason that I can now look back and classify our actions as mistakes is because these were rushed decisions; we didn't think them through. We moved with our flesh first, acting on what felt good to us at the moment. We made decisions based upon what we wanted. We never prayed, individually or together, to ask God for permission or guidance, about the situation. We never even asked God the simple question, "Lord, is he/she for me?"

I had simply assumed that because I wanted a man, God had blessed me with one. Never did I consider that the enemy could have packaged a handsome gift just for me for a specific purpose: to try to break me! Little did I know at the time that the enemy's goal with this hurried relationship was to distract me and pull me away from cultivating an intimate relationship with the Savior.

I had once been told by a wise woman that when a man seeks his wife, she should be so consumed in doing the work of the Lord that she would not even notice anyone looking at her. At this point in my life, I can honestly admit that this was not my truth. I was too busy looking around and watching to see who was looking at me. When Justin looked at me, I immediately caught his gaze and fell right into it.

My daughter Sierra's father, Nigel, had recently married and was consistently active in her life. Nigel had also known Justin from childhood, as they had lived in the same neighborhood. Nigel was fully supportive of my new relationship with Justin. On the other hand, the mother of Justin's two children was not exactly jumping with excitement about our new relationship, understandably. I will not go into details, but I think you get the picture. Unbeknownst to me at the time, he still had some things going on with her. This would manifest into an issue in the very near future.

Writing on the Wall

Prior to Justin and I meeting, he had gone to prison for a domestic violence situation. According to the Bureau of Justice statistics, one in three black men can expect to go to prison in their lifetime. In several states, at least one in 20 adult black males is in prison. In my mind, it was necessary for me to dismiss the fact that he had gone to prison; I chose to believe that Justin was just another black man who had been unfairly targeted through the unfair and discriminatory practices of the criminal justice system. The reality was that I was just making excuses for what I wanted, because nothing else really mattered to me at that time.

Rather than paying attention to the writing on the wall, I allowed myself to find comfort in simply saying, "No one is perfect. The black man gets railroad daily just because of his race." However, the truth was that my self-esteem was at an all-time low. It was so low, in fact, that I convinced myself not to acknowledge that there was a problem, despite the clear warning signs that were right there before me. Knowing the unhealthy state of my esteem, the enemy entered in and convinced me to justify them, to ignore them. That's exactly what I did.

I had stocked my mind full of justifications and excuses for why I could have a good relationship with someone who had been legally convicted and imprisoned for domestic violence. First, I was one of those women who said, "Domestic violence? That would never happen to me. I'm not like the women that he dealt with before. I am different!"

Then, I leaned on what I thought was the strength of our love. I convinced myself that the love we shared was stronger and greater than any love that either of us had ever experienced. Because of this powerful, never-before-experienced love that we shared, he would never dare put his hands on me. Those other relationships in which he had committed domestic violence were in his past; I was his future, and the love of his lifetime.

Finally, my all-time favorite excuse was, "He's changed!" I would tell myself, and others, that there is no shame on people who have changed, because God is a restorer. God does not charge our past to us; He forgives us and tells us to "Go and sin no more." This is exactly what I believed Justin had done. Now that he was with me, he was a changed man. The things that he had done before were things of the past, and they would never manifest again, especially with me.

Mind you, these were all thoughts and imaginations, justification that I'd manufactured in my own mind. I had no evidence to back them. I hadn't actually observed his behavior over time and made these evaluations based on what I saw in him. I never confirmed that my beliefs about how much of a changed man he was were actually true. Instead, I simply chose to believe that he had been restored from his past, without any reason other than wanting to believe it.

I had what I felt at the time was a good reason to accept the ideas that I had conjured up about a "brand new Justin." The reason: we *really* wanted each other, so we were moving with urgency... with a whirlwind force and an unapologetically fast pace. After all, we had professed our love for one another, and this shared love felt good to both of us. It was our love that mattered, not the facts. Oh, how I wish I had taken the time to pay attention to the writing on the wall.

Even though Justin and I had been going strong for months as girlfriend and boyfriend, we'd had our fair share of arguments and disagreements. I wouldn't say that we had an excessive number of disagreements; it was just the normal stuff that people in relationships disagree about. However, the disagreements that we had were nothing compared to the ones that I witnessed him having with his kids' mother over the phone. When he and she argued it was *brutal*! I mean, he called out of her name constantly, and she would do the same, both of them yelling at the top of their lungs and each trying to make their feelings heard.

As I watched their heated exchanges, I would just shake my head, saying to myself, "Hell, no! That would *never* be me! He would *never* disrespect me in that fashion. He loves me! They just have a toxic relationship, and all of this is has to be her fault. Why is she intentionally inciting him and pushing his buttons in such a way?”

Writing on the Wall

The way Justin’s face contorted when he was angry was disturbing. He no longer looked like my handsome boyfriend. Instead, he looked damn near demonic, for a lack of a better description. His eyes became a bloodshot red. On top of his nose were small beads of sweat, and from his forehead down to his neck, he was drenched in sweat. The rage in him was strong and undeniable. In a dysfunctional way, I kind of took pride that I was the only one who could seem to calm him down when his anger escalated to that level of recklessness.

Months passed in our happy relationship. I became pregnant, and Justin and I were excited about this new blessing in our lives. However, we did not share this news with my parents yet, because I was very ill. My thought was, “Let me get through the hard part of the pregnancy, and when I feel stronger, I will let my parents know about it.” I thought that would be best.

My reasoning for delaying the announcement of my pregnancy to my mother and father was that my parents are from the islands; they’re Caribbean parents. Anyone who was raised by parents from the islands *completely* understand what I mean! Let me be clear: I am Americanized, but my upbringing was strongly influenced by my Caribbean heritage. It was always emphasized in my life as being an integral part of the fabric that I was cut from, and my parents made sure that I honored it always! I am thankful to my parents for instilling this in me and my siblings as well as their grandchildren.

Writing on the Wall

My parents liked Justin as a person, and they were always gracious and respectful to him. However, they did make it clear to me in private settings that he was not their choice for me. Justin and I had come from different cultures and backgrounds. When my parents voiced these concerns, their words were not meant to be digs at Justin, and they did not mean any offense to him or his family. They were simply acknowledging that he and I were just not cut from the same cloth. Biblically speaking, we were not equally yoked.

❧

My mother, the matriarch of my family, was a member of the British Air Force in England as a young woman. She moved to Canada after leaving the Air Force and met and fell in love with my biological father, a six-foot tall, reddish-brown, handsome Jamaican man. He was not as educated and polished as my mother, but she wanted a man. You see, like me, my mother had a seven year-old son from a prior relationship, an old boyfriend she met during her early days in England. She married the handsome Jamaican, who would five years later become my biological father, against my grandparents' advice. They had reservations about my mother's choice and did not approve of her marriage. Little did I know that this would be a pattern that I would eventually follow later in life.

Not long after they were married, my biological father became physically, emotionally and verbally abusive to my mother. Although I never witnessed the physical abuse first-hand, I can recall the arguments and ugly words that he yelled at my mother. As if this behavior was not vile enough, he also had the nerve to be a habitual cheater. I saw the parade of women that he cruelly introduced me and my older brother to on a regular basis. Despite the violence that persisted in their relationship, my mother and father, who already had my mother's son from a former relationship, would go on to have another son, and then me, the youngest of my three siblings and the only girl.

In the beginning of my parents' relationship, my mother said that my father had been a good stepfather to my oldest brother. However, when my brother started to mature and his features began to resemble those of his biological father's, my father began to be mean-spirited and cold towards him. Of course, this bothered my mother, and it became a source of constant conflict between them.

The discord that characterized my parents' relationship eventually began to wear on my mom. My mom, who stood at a mere 4'11", was very petite. She was beautiful both inside and outside, hands down. Even though she had been bullied and disrespected throughout the relationship by my father, one thing that she would not tolerate was him doing the same thing to her baby.

My mom had become an expert at concealing the evidence of my father's destructive ways towards her. She covered up bruises, heartache and pain. Although she was embarrassed and ashamed about what was happening to her behind closed doors, she had not yet reached her breaking point. Many years later, however, she would enter into an intimate relationship with the Lord. Empowered by the newfound strength of this spiritual relationship, she would eventually muster up the strength to flee Canada, leaving behind a destructive relationship with her kids and her dignity in tow. Off we went to California, just my mother, me, and my two brothers, embarking on a new beginning in life.

It was here in California that my mother rekindled her relationship with her true love. You see, while my mother was in the British Air Force as a young woman, before she'd left England and moved to Canada, she'd met an intelligent, loving, caring young man who was also in the Air Force at the time. There in England, the two fell in love. However, he was not just a boyfriend; he had been the love of her life!

His name was Mitch. Like my mother, Mitch also met a woman after leaving the Air Force, fell in love and gotten married. From that union, he had a son. Years later, Mitch and his wife were divorced. By God's grace, both my mother and Mitch had both kept in contact with a mutual friend from their days in England, and this person played a key role in reuniting them.

Shortly after they were reunited in California, my mom and Mitch were married. This was one of the biggest blessings of my life, because it allowed me the fortunate opportunity to witness how a man is truly supposed to love a woman. In turn, I saw my mom experience the true love and friendship that she deserved.

This union was also a tremendous blessing in my own life. Today, when I refer to my "father," I am not referring to my biological father; I am referring to Mitch. He is much more than a stepfather; He is truly my dad. Together, my mom and dad provided me with an amazing life. I was raised in the middle class. In my family, education was a must and etiquette was a lifestyle. Pride in our Jamaican culture was the foundation of my upbringing.

Justin's parents have been married for over 50 years now; they had been married for 40 years when Justin and I had begun dating. They met when they were young; his father was in the army and later retired from the post office. His mother was a jack-of-all-trades. I fondly remember a lot of wonderful stories that she shared with me about her younger years, especially about all of the parties that she'd gone to and the fun she'd had.

Justin's parents had only two children, both boys. Justin was the youngest, like me. Justin's own upbringing was similar to the stories about her own upbringing that his mother told. His family was filled with so much life! They enjoyed taking fun trips as a family, and his parents spent lots of quality family time with their kids. Justin's upbringing sounded like a blast!

Despite the fun times that they shared as a family, like many marriages, Justin's parents experienced problems, including affairs and abuse. Both Justin and his mother shared these accounts with me; I never actually witnessed them. However, from the stories they told, it became clear to me that Justin and I had encountered some of the same problematic issues in our upbringing and witnessed some of the same patterns in our respective environments.

❧

Seven months into our relationship, an incident occurred, which I can still recall vividly. One of my best friends was preparing to celebrate her wedding, the same girlfriend that was with me when I first crossed paths with Justin at the store after many years. Another one of my best friends had also flown in to attend the wedding. It was going to be a wonderful celebration, and Justin and I were super excited to be attending it.

I was still living with my parents at the time, but they were out of town during the time of the big wedding weekend; they regularly travel the world together. Since they were not at the house and I was pregnant and still very sick, Justin would come over and spend the night with me, trying his best to comfort me.

Four days before the wedding, Justin came over as usual. However, that night, he was clearly stressed out. He'd had a lot of trouble at home with his brother, his parents, and his brother's live-in girlfriend. He wouldn't go into too much detail. All he would tell me was that they kept having huge, blown-up arguments, and that he couldn't afford to violate his parole. Apparently, when someone is on parole, they have to stay completely out of trouble. They can't even be *accused* of anything, even if it's just a general complaint.

That night, Justin didn't sleep a wink. He was up the majority of the night, pacing. I later discovered that what he had failed to mention to me was that his parole officer had called him and told him to come into the office for a meeting. This was strange because his parole officer usually came to Justin's parents' house for their appointments.

An hour before his 9 a.m. appointment, Justin became nervous, so nervous that he started crying and throwing up. He kept calling his friends and asking for their opinion. I tried to console him as much as possible. I thought he was overreacting; he hadn't told me the details of what had really happened, so I couldn't understand what the big deal was. Justin rolled a blunt, asked to borrow my car, kissed me on my forehead, and left.

One hour passed. I thought that now would be a good time to call and check on him and find out how his meeting went. His phone went straight to his voicemail. *Hmm, that's strange.* I thought. *Maybe he is calling me at the same time. That's happened before.* I smiled and then waited for a few minutes. No phone call. I dialed his number again. Once again, it went straight to his voicemail without ringing. His phone was turned off. But why?

Before I could even begin to worry, my daughter and nephew came into my bedroom asking for breakfast.

"One sec," I said. "Let me make this phone call and I will feed you two, okay?"

"Okay!" they replied in unison. My daughter was just about to make a special breakfast request when the phone rang. I held up my finger signaling for her to hold the thought.

"One moment!" I said to her. She knew what that meant, so she closed the door and I answered the phone. "Hello?"

"Yes, I am looking for a Brea Hill," the authoritative but friendly male voice responded on the other end.

"Oh, it's *Bree*. Who is calling?" I asked.

He glossed over the correction and said, "This is Officer Jones. We have your car at the station. It needs to be picked up ASAP or it will be towed."

"Wait, what? Where is my boyfriend, Justin? Why would you tow it?" I was confused.

"He has been detained," the officer stated.

"Why?" I asked. I was trying not to panic.

"I am not at liberty to disclose that, but he asked me to call you about your car, and I told him I would," the officer explained.

"Officer, please! I love him! We are expecting a *child*! Please, Sir. I *need* to know about him!" I could tell that Officer Jones was beginning to feel a bit sympathetic.

"All I can say is that he has violated his parole and they have him detained for the violation." *Parole hold?* I thought. The tears began to flow as the officer continued. "Come down to the office. We have your keys, and you may get some additional information."

I wiped the tears from my face and held my stomach, just as I felt a sharp pain. I immediately started to get ready to go to the station.

Opening the door, I yelled downstairs to my daughter and nephew, "Eat some cereal quickly then get dressed! We have to make a run!" All I heard was the sound of sucking teeth.

"Cereal?" they both called back with irritated voices.

"Yes, and hurry up now!" I yelled back. They could tell that I was not in a good mood, and from then until the time we left the house, they tiptoed around me accordingly.

I called one of Justin's friends to come and pick me up and take me to the police station to get my car. As soon as he arrived, I made it clear to him that I wanted to keep the matter as quiet as possible, not discussing it in front of the kids; there was no need for them to be concerned with the details of such an adult situation. It was a very quiet ride.

As we pulled up to the police station, I saw my car sitting there in the parking lot. I thanked Justin's friend for the ride, and the kids and I jumped out of the car.

Walking into the station, I instantly became both anxious and nauseated. I had never seen a parole office before, *ever*! I had always been sheltered from such things throughout my upbringing; no one from my immediate family had ever been in trouble with the law to such a degree.

When we entered into the lobby, a man came out of a conference room. He asked, "May I help you?" I instantly recognized his voice from our earlier conversation over the phone.

"Officer Jones?"

"Yes," he replied. "It's Bree, correct?" I smiled with acknowledgement that he had gotten the pronunciation of my name correct this time. "Come this way," he said. He led me and the kids to a conference room.

When we walked into room 11, there stood a petite, light-skinned black lady with blonde hair. Her small stature reminded me of my mother; however, unlike my mom, this lady was not friendly at all. She seemed to completely lack any personality or social skills. From the authoritative way in which she conducted herself, I could clearly tell that she had a lot of power in that office.

The lady coldly instructed us to have a seat, and we did. Then, she immediately launched into a series of questions, interrogating me. There was no opening dialogue with this lady, not even an introduction of who she was before she began to question me as if I was a criminal.

Offended at her approach, rather than respond to her questions, I took a moment to, very tactfully, let her know who I was and who I was not. My guess was that since I was sitting in a police station, she had assumed that I was a person who lived the kind of life that gave her permission to treat me with disrespect. Thus, I explained to her that I was not one of those 'common women' who is on public assistance with multiple kids and no education and that I would appreciate if she did not stereotype or treat me as such.

Unmoved by my mini speech, she continued with her line of questioning.

"Can you tell me why he was arrested?" I asked with humility in a calm tone.

"He is a Peeping Tom," she said bluntly. Her words were chilling and rocked me to my core. From that point until the time we left the police station, everything would seem to move in slow motion. *Clearly this woman had the wrong person in custody,* I thought. *What was wrong with her? She had to be freaking delusional*!

Without missing a beat, the woman looked at my daughter and asked, "Is she your daughter?" I could see the accusation in her eyes as her gaze fixed on her.

Now, this chick has lost her damn mind! I thought. "Yes, she is," I replied defensively, sensing her allegation. "What does that have to do with anything?" I couldn't believe that this woman was doing this. I had been talking about my man and this woman had randomly brought up my baby girl!

"You need to be careful with him around her," she warned. I cast a venomous glare at the woman. If looks could kill, she would have keeled over and dropped dead at that moment.

My response was spoken in a tone that was meant for her to clearly understand that she had just openly offended me in front of my kids.

"First of all, I will *not* have these *lies* about my man freely come out of your mouth in front of my kids. So let's you and I have a discussion kid-free. I need to have them go to the front and sit in the lobby. Would that be okay?" I asked.

"I don't think that's a good idea, Ms. Hill. This is a parole office," she replied condescendingly at my naïveté. She continued, "The people out in the lobby are not nice people.

You have pedophiles, molesters, rapists, murderers, and robbers sitting outside in that lobby."

I honestly felt like I was in a bad nightmare. I would have done anything for someone – hell, *anyone* – to wake me up.

Writing on the Wall

Justin had already served time in jail before we began our relationship, and I had dismissed it as an isolated incident that had happened once in his life. Now, he was in jail – again. This was the cold, hard reality that was staring me in the face. However, the coldest part about the situation was not that it was reality; it was that this was *my* reality. *I* was living a nightmare.

It was time for me to pull myself together and ask the difficult questions. "What is he being accused of?" I asked the woman.

"He was accused of peeping at a family member," she replied. She went on to explain that one of his family members had said that he was watching them and reported the accusation to his parole officer.

To make matters worse, the woman also explained that Justin's ex-girlfriend, the one with whom he had recently ended his relationship, had also reportedly filed a restraining order against him, another incident that he had not disclosed to me. When Justin had explained to me that he "needed to tie up some loose strings," with her, I assumed that he had done exactly that. No questions asked. Clearly that was a mistake on my part.

After having my questions answered, the kids and I left the parole office. I felt drained and overwhelmed. Once we hopped in my car, I remember looking over my shoulder at my daughter in the back seat to catch a glimpse of her body language; I needed to know how she was feeling after hearing such a disturbing mouthful about my boyfriend. She looked disturbed and confused. However, rather than offer her words of comfort and consolation, I didn't say a word. Some part of me hoped that by some miracle, she did not take everything in that was said in the parole office. Yeah, right.

We made the drive home from the police station in as much silence as there was on the drive to the station earlier that day. I was not feeling well at all. Ever since the phone call that I had received that morning telling me to come down to the parole office, I had been experiencing the worst cramps ever. However, I could not concentrate on them earlier; I was too distracted with trying to hold my world together, which seemed to be crumbling right before me.

When I got home, all I could do was cry myself to sleep. I honestly don't even remember if my nephew and daughter ate dinner that night. All I remember is that, as I lay in my bed, I comforted myself with the assurance that if they got hungry enough, they would just eat some cereal. My honest truth at that moment was that I was not trying to win any Mother or Aunt-of-the-Year awards. Instead, I was selfishly buried in my own feelings of depression and despair. The devil had to be happy that night.

It was 7:27 a.m. the next morning. Ring, ring, ring...

"Hello?" I answered tiredly.

The automated lady's voice on the other end said, "You have received a collect call from Justin, an inmate at the Los Angeles County Jail." Everything was spoken in the automated lady's voice except his name, which had been recorded in his own voice, which seemed filled with distress. I accepted the call without hesitation.

"Hey babe," he said.

"Justin," I responded softly, almost in an infant's tone. "What is happening? This lady told me all sorts of things about you. Are they true? Are you okay? I'm scared!" I asked, not even pausing to let him answer in between questions. I was frustrated and confused, seeking answers to questions that I had been tossing around in my head all night. I wanted him to assure me that, despite everything that had happened, everything was going to be alright.

"I don't even know why I'm in here. This is bogus." His voice was calm.

"They said that you're a Peeping Tom!" I blurted out.

"What the hell? That is a lie! Baby, this is all a misunderstanding."

"Then why are you locked up?" I asked.

He quickly responded, "Because I am on parole! When you're on parole, it's like you're the property of the State. You can't have a complaint against you or be accused of anything when you are on parole, no matter what. So technically, because someone lied on me and made a formal complaint to my PO, I'm stuck!" He paused and then continued, "Babe, I feel so alone. We are supposed to be getting ready to celebrate Scharae's wedding! Now the pigs have me in this trick bag because folks are jealous of our relationship." His argument sounded credible.

"How long can they hold you?" I asked.

"I'm not sure. I have to talk to my public defender when I get my day in court." Throughout the rest of the call, he mockingly referred to his court-appointed lawyer as the "public pretender."

I admitted to Justin that this entire situation was a whole new world for me. It felt like he was speaking a foreign language, and I could pick up on his frustration that I was unable to keep up with all of the correctional system jargon and the details that he was trying to explain regarding the legal process.

"This is too much for me," I said. "What about the baby?" The thought of having *another* child out of wedlock, with *another* man, was sickening. Plus, I had my parents to think about. *Damn!* I thought. *My parents are already going to kill me once they find out I'm pregnant, and now the ol' boy who is the father is in jail*!

Before he could answer my question, the automated lady's voice interrupted, saying, "You are speaking to an inmate in the Los Angeles County Jail." Each time I heard that random automated reminder about who I was speaking to and where he was, it made me sick to my stomach. We both paused silently until the automated lady had finished her message.

"I have to go," Justin said. "I will call you soon to explain everything. I love you! *Please* don't abandon me. I need you in my dark time. *Please* don't take me away from our baby. Promise me you won't leave me?" he begged anxiously. Before I could respond to such a huge plea, the phone call was disconnected.

❧

It was the big wedding weekend, and my two besties, Mia and Scharae, and I would soon be together again, reunited for the festivities. However, the recent events that had occurred with Justin cast a dark shadow over what was supposed to be a time of joyous celebration and non-stop fun. I knew that I would have to spill the details of what was happening in my life, and I wondered about their responses.

The dynamics of my two besties are like night and day. The one common thread is that we are all best friends together, even though their two personalities differ. Scharae (the bride-to-be) is very sweet, a social butterfly, and very politically correct. She is also very tactful; she has the gift of choosing just the right words to let you know that something probably is not a great decision or good idea, followed by one of her favorite lines: "But, I kind of understand why you might feel that way." As the person on the receiving end of her advice, you don't feel foolish or judged. Her approach makes receiving great advice that much easier. She gives you the bitter with the sweet, and because of her approach, you feel comfortable disclosing everything to her.

On the other hand, Mia, aka "The Guard Dog," is a bit different. Mia is suspicious; she considers anyone who comes around our friendship trio to be a suspect, until they are proven otherwise. Mia has a great discerning spirit, and she has to get a good feel for someone's personality before she will let her guard down around them. Our sacred sisterhood spanning more than 25 years is sacred to her, and she is very protective of it. Although Mia is tactful, she is also a shoot-from-the-hip, call-it-like-I-see-it kind of woman; when she weighs in on something, you will clearly know where she stands, because she does not leave any room for misunderstanding.

The bottom line is that my besties, who I consider to be my sisters, and I love one another immensely. However, we also make sure that we are truthful in sharing our feelings about anything and everything. When we first met, little did I know that these two beautiful women would play a major role in my life in years to come, as well as in my daughter's life: they are both her godmothers. When the time came for me to select which of my besties would take on the role of being her godmother, I couldn't choose between one or the other, so I appointed them both! It was the best decision of my life. It's comforting to know I didn't always make bad choices.

My bestie, Mia, who had flown out to California for Scharae's wedding, came over to my house later on the same day that I'd received Justin's phone call from jail. I began to tell her everything, from the accusation that the woman at the police station made about Justin, to the pregnancy, to him now being in jail on a probation violation, or "parole hold" as he so casually called it.

I remember that after hearing about everything that was happening with Justin and me, Mia looked me straight in my eyes and said, "He is not right for you." She did not follow her statement up with anything else – not a word. In fact, we sat in awkward silence after she made that direct statement about the love of my life. I wanted to hit her!

"So what are you going to do?" Mia asked after giving me several moments to digest her candid, direct response. Before I could respond, she followed her question with a statement. "Jail means we broke up!" she said.

I chuckled a bit because my besties and I had always said that if we ever dealt with a man that found himself in jail while we were in a relationship, it would automatically mean that "We broke up!" However, at the present moment, this was more than just one of our funny sayings. It was a critical, real-life decision I was facing. I was in love with this man and we were expecting a baby together. I was banking on his story about being falsely accused being true so that we could soon be reunited, and I would no longer be in the position of having to make such a heart-wrenching decision.

In hindsight, I wish I had been strong enough at that moment to say, "Jail means we broke up," and mean it. I wish I'd had the ability to stick to the promise to walk away, a promise that I had made when I was in my right mind, rather than backtrack on that promise out of a mindset that was clouded with emotion, desperation, and a baby to come. Unfortunately, as my parents frequently said when I was a child, a hard head makes for a soft butt!

The next morning, I received another collect call from the county jail. This time, Justin's voice was unrecognizable, void of the sexy tone, charm and swag to which I had always been drawn.

"We need to speak quick," he said, hastily explaining that his time on the phone was limited. He told me that he had gone to court and that he had pleaded innocent to the charges brought against him. As per Justin, they did not have any evidence to convict him of the charges. However, because he was accused of a possible crime while on parole, he had to do eight months for the violation. Over and over, he confessed his love for me and our baby and begged me to be there for him. He said that he would be home very shortly and make things up to me and our baby.

Despite the feeling in the pit of my stomach that was screaming *Hell, no!*, in my brokenness, I said, "Okay, I will be there for you."

I desperately wanted to believe that the only man that has professed his love for me was being truthful and that he had been falsely accused because of all the haters in his life that were jealous of our relationship. What I would learn in the years to come was that the feeling I'd felt in the pit of my stomach, the feeling that was pulling at my *core*, was Jesus trying to get my attention. However, because I never brought this issue to the Lord, choosing to operate out of my own will rather than out of God the King's will, He allowed things to transpire in my life.

Writing on the Wall

One week later, after I had agreed to "rock with" Justin (maintain my relationship with him) through his storm, I encountered my first personal storm. I lost the baby. The one major reason that was keeping us together was gone, but still, I stayed.

two

Calendar

Following the devastating loss of the baby, I took a two-week leave of absence from work to recuperate physically, mentally and emotionally. After the two weeks, although I still wasn't a hundred percent, I knew that I had to muster up the strength to go back to my job working as a call center agent at a Fortune 500 company. Getting back to work was especially necessary now that I had acquired some new expenses; there were excessive collect calls from Justin, and I also had to put money on his books and send him care packages on top of my own regular bills and living expenses. I managed the burden of these new financial demands the best I could, because I felt that it was my responsibility to do so. Providing financial support was my way of showing him – proving to him – that I would not abandon him while he was behind bars.

It was ironic. Being in a relationship with a man who was locked up was depressing. It felt like I was locked up, too, because in a sense, my freedom had been taken away. I didn't feel free to come and go as I pleased. I felt the pressure to ensure that I was always available to receive his phone calls. I constantly felt guilty about having fun and living a normal life. I found myself pretending that I was miserable and disguising the fun that I would be feeling when he called, just so I wouldn't hurt his feelings or make him angry at me for having fun without him. It was *very* draining. I was not aware of it then, but in retrospect, I realize that I was learning, even mastering, how to hide, cover-up, and camouflage things in my life at will. The seed was sown way back then.

Dealing with Justin's issues and problems consumed me, leaving me feeling overloaded and mentally, emotionally and financially drained. It eventually began to take a toll on me, even affecting me socially. For example, there were a few times when I was approached by or had a conversation with a good looking, professional man; you know, the type that you could proudly take home to your mama. They would openly express their interest in getting to know me better on a personal level. Of course, the loyal and faithful girlfriend that I was, I would openly disclose that I was with someone – and he was in jail. As soon as this was revealed, they would look at me like, "Are you serious?" and exit stage right in a hurry.

Little did I realize that they knew something that even I did not realize about myself: my self-esteem was at an all-time low. When a man or woman with healthy self-esteem senses that they might be dealing with a potential partner who has unhealthy, low self-esteem, they take off running in the opposite direction. They see the warning signs and flee! In my case, I didn't even see the warning signs in my own life. Low self-esteem can sometimes speak more loudly than your own intuitive warning center, convincing you to believe that you are not worthy of anything good – including a good, respectable partner who is kind, responsible, and full of integrity. In my case, because of my low self-esteem, I thought that the man who I was financially and emotionally supporting while he was behind bars, a man who was locked up for reasons I could not even bear to think about without becoming sick to my stomach, and a man who obviously has some dangling relationship issues with another woman, was the best that I deserved.

❧

We talked on the phone a lot. Over the course of seven days, we probably spoke for four or five of them – that is, if the facility was not on lockdown. During lockdown periods, the inmates were not allowed to communicate with the outside world. The eight-month jail sentence seemed to pass fairly quickly for me, although I am sure that Justin might have had a different opinion, considering that he was the one actually serving the time. Before I knew it, "we" were already at the seven-month mark, exactly 30 days before he was to return to me.

Justin was so fired up about his imminent release! He was so ready to start his new life and make good on all of the promises he had showered me with in the beginning. I was also looking forward to him fulfilling his promises and obligations to me. I had "rocked with him" throughout what seemed to be his darkest time, but now that there was a light at the end of the tunnel, I was looking forward to feeling free again myself.

A part of me was a bit nervous about Justin's release, because we'd actually spent the majority of our relationship apart due to his legal situation. We'd missed out on a lot of the "firsts" that characterize normal relationships like the bliss of the honeymoon period, first arguments, celebrating our anniversary, and sharing the holidays with one another. We would never get that time back. We would also never have a relationship that was not tainted by the dead weight of him going to jail. Therefore, our relationship was not like the average relationship; there was a lot about it that would not be considered "normal." It was almost like we would have to start learning about each other all over again when he was released, because we had not done so properly at the start of our relationship.

Another part of me recognized that I would gain a lot of "hood credit" for being that "down chick" because of the way that I had supported Justin while he was in jail; I "held it down" for him for his entire bid. This would have been a bonus if I had been "hood," but I was not. It would also have been beneficial if I had desired to be seen as a "down chick," but this also did not particularly interest me. I had grown up in a middle-class neighborhood with a polished and cultured family. There was nothing "hood" about me, and I did not have any "hood" aspirations. Because of this, Justin considered me "bougie." To me, this was not a bad thing. The truth of the matter is that we were total opposites who were forcefully merging our lives and lifestyles together.

The big day had come: it was the date for Justin to be released. *Finally!* I thought. I was *over the moon* excited about being together with him again. The plan was for me to drive to San Diego, pick him up, and bring him back home. I rented a car for the weekend because I didn't want to put a lot of additional miles on my own car. Fortunately, Scharae had agreed to make the two hour ride to San Diego with me; I was both relieved and excited that she could make the trip. After all, she and her husband were still newlyweds at the time. I made sure to thank her husband sincerely for being super cool about allowing his new wifey to accompany me.

My partner in crime, Scharae, and I jumped on the road. As soon as we merged onto the freeway, I excitedly yelled, "Road trip!" at the top of my voice. I felt exuberant and liberated. We headed to San Diego, all smiles.

We made it to the hotel in record time; in my haste to get to San Diego as quickly as I could, I had floored it! I was giddy. In less than 24 hours, I would be reunited with my love! I would be able to kiss, love on, and make love to the man whom I thought was the man of dreams. I probably only slept about a solid three hours in preparation for the big reunion.

The next morning, I woke up super early. I wanted to take my time getting ready, because I needed to ensure that I was fly and sexy looking for Justin. What was ironic was that within the past eight months, I couldn't remember having said a single prayer, having been so consumed with our relationship drama. However, that morning I had a strange notion to say a prayer, so I did exactly that. It is so easy to acknowledge God when we are happy and feeling that we are getting our way. It's borderline effortless.

I guess all my bumping around in the hotel room caused Scharae to wake up. She looked over at me.

"Today is the day, huh?" she asked in a half-sleepy voice.

"Yup!" I answered in a cheerful tone.

In a sarcastic but joking manner, she said, "Hell, who put a nickel in you last night? I wanted to drop some Nyquil in your drink so bad. You were so dang hyper, talking a mile a minute with your anxious butt!"

We both laughed. I had to agree that I had been "Talky Tina" the whole night through! In fact, Scharae had actually gone to sleep on me while I was talking to her. It didn't hurt my feelings one bit; she is known for getting cozy, rubbing her feet together, and then knocking out. It is actually a running joke between me, Mia and Scharae. Once we notice that Scharae is rubbing her feet together, we all know that she will soon be out for the count.

The drive to the facility was nerve wracking. I had all sorts of thoughts and questions running rampant through my mind. *What if we were not attracted to each other again? What if he harbored bad feelings against me for the loss of our baby? What if he had lost his swag and charm that I was attracted to? What if he had become institutionalized, going back and forth to jail?* I shook my head back and forth as if I was literally trying to shake all of these questions and concerns out of my head.

We pulled up to the inmate release holding area. In the distance, I could see a white van driving about 15 miles per hour and headed in our direction. I knew we were in the right area, as I saw other cars parked there with people who were also waiting. They wore a variety of expressions, some with anxious faces, some smiling, some crying, and some blank-faced, as if this was an all-too-familiar pick-up. The white van got closer and closer, until it pulled up and parked directly beside us. One by one, the released inmates began to exit the van. I felt the flutter of butterflies inside, and my stomach began to do cartwheels.

We sat in the car and watched each inmate climb out of the van. However, by the time about seven of the inmates had been released, headed directly to the embrace of their waiting loved ones, I did not see Justin. *Where is he?* I thought. I mentally checked the date to ensure that I had it right.

At this point, I began to quietly mumble to myself, "I know I have my dates right. Hell, I'd better! I took off from work, and rented a car and all!" Again, it felt like I was moving in slow motion. It was the same feeling I had felt when I had gone to the parole office.

In a panic, I began to fumble for my purse to pull out Justin's inmate information. If he did not get off that van, I was surely going to walk over to speak with the officer who was driving to find out what in the hell was going on!

While my head was down as I searched for the paperwork in my purse with near hysteria, Scharae said, "There he is!"

Before I could even look up and confirm it for myself, a sense of calmness had overtaken me. A huge smile was instantly plastered on my face as I grinned from ear to ear!

I looked up, and my eyes connected with Justin's as he walked towards the car. He had a big smile on his face, too. When he reached the car, I opened the door and embraced him passionately. I took the whole moment in, breathing in deeply and exhaling the familiar smell of my love, which I had sorely missed over the past eight months.

He looked so handsome! A month prior, I had sent him a care package. In it was a new outfit for him to wear on his release date, also known in prison verbiage (which I was forced to learn with much reluctance) as "dress out." Justin was known for his "grown man" attire, so I wanted to make sure that I kept it going. He was wearing a nice pair of dark denim jeans, hard-bottomed Stacy Adams shoes, and a button-down, collared shirt. His hair was freshly cut, his waves defined, and his goatee lined to perfection. There is just something about a even-toned dark-complexioned man to me. Chocolate was my *weakness*! I was pleased to see Justin in the outfit that I had picked out for him.

After our embrace, Justin gently held my face in his hands, drew me close, and gently kissed me first on my forehead and then my neck. Then, he whispered so softly in my ear, "I'm happy to be home. I love you." His rhythm for the kiss and affectionate words were impeccable.

"Damn!" I said to myself as I melted in his arms. I could not wait to be alone with him and allow him to handle me to the best of his abilities. It been a long eight months, and my body was calling!

Scharae got out of the car and gave Justin a hug. "Hey brother," she said affectionately.

"Hey sis! Thanks for being a true 'road dawg' to my girl," he said.

"It's all good," Scharae replied. "Now let's get on the road. I'm starting to miss my hubby now!"

I excitedly jumped into the back seat with Justin.

"Oh, so I'm the chauffeur, huh?" Scharae asked. "Just kidding! Sit back and relax. I got this!" With that, we proceeded towards the freeway and headed for home.

In Justin's arms, I was so content, so much so that he and I both fell asleep right there in the back seat. I guess the lack of sleep the night before had finally caught up with me, and evidently, with him, too.

The car came to a complete stop. "We're here!" Scharae announced.

Justin and I woke up, looked at each other and smiled. Both of us were secretly happy that we were not dreaming. Our present reality was that our nightmare was over. Now, it was time for us to reset our relationship and get back on track.

Rather than me returning to my parents' house, Justin and I went to a hotel room for the remainder of the weekend.

Upon our arrival at the hotel, I called my parents to check on my baby girl. She was having fun with her grandparents, who spoiled her to no end. I gave her my love and told her I would be back tomorrow afternoon.

After I got off the phone with Sierra, I turned to talk to Justin. I had a lot of unanswered questions, and this was the first moment that he and I had truly had a chance to be alone with no distractions. It seemed like the right time to delve into a serious discussion of my concerns. There was never any time like the present to address such things, right?

Justin, on the other hand, had another agenda planned, and his agenda superseded my own.

"We have all the time in the world to talk," he said, putting off my request for conversation for a later time. Right then, he wanted me. I reached for my purse and pulled out a condom. I wanted to be prepared this time. He tossed it aside.

"I don't want to get pregnant again," I whispered.

"Trust me, you won't," he assured me. We began to make passionate love to each other. It was incredible!

The next morning when we woke up, I again began to initiate a conversation about our future and what had happened in the past. He cut me off mid-sentence.

"Babe, we can discuss all of that tonight," he said, irritated. "Right now, I have to meet up with my parole officer before I miss the deadline to check in with him."

Apparently, when you are a newly-released inmate, you have 48 hours from the date of your release to check in with your parole officer (PO), or they can charge you with a violation of not following protocol. Of course, such a violation would mean that his legal issues would overshadow our relationship, and I did not want to go through those shenanigans again.

Justin also mentioned that after his meeting with his PO, he needed to go see his parents and his kids. He went to each of these meetings alone, without me. I dropped him off at his parole office and told him to call me later. Then, I headed home to my daughter, whom I dearly missed.

Later that night, Justin called me and said that he was exhausted. After his meeting with his PO, he had spent the entire rest of the day with his kids, and all of this activity had tired him out. He said that he was calling it a night and that he would see me in the morning.

"So you don't have enough energy to speak with me? I've been trying to have a real discussion with you, and each time, you've managed to not acknowledge my feelings," I said.

"Quit overreacting, man!" he responded. "Why are you tripping? You are acting like the CO in jail! I told you about what happened. They lied on me. Period! The reason why I was in there is because I was on parole. I pleaded innocent to the lies, but still they were able to violate me because of my circumstances. I don't want to keep talking about this. I don't look in the rearview mirror. I move forward."

Before I could say a word about the guilt trip he was trying to lay at my feet, I heard a child's voice say, "Daddy, Mommy wants you to come here."

"Oh! So you're with your baby mama," I immediately responded in a very facetious tone. Justin knew that I hated that term.

"So now I'm not allowed to be by my kids' mom's?" he asked.

"I never once said that," I replied. "However, you were so dog tired a few minutes ago, I'd assumed you were at your parents house alone."

"Good night. We will talk in the morning," was all he said back to me.

"Maybe not!" I shouted. Then, I hung up the phone. I kept thinking to myself, *He is the king of flipping things around! How did he manage to make me feel guilty when he was the one that omitted the truth?* This was a pattern that I would, unfortunately, grow used to experiencing.

The next morning, I intentionally did not answer any of Justin's phone calls. Instead, my daughter and I went out and had a blast! As we hung out, I realized that she and I had not been spending as much time together as we used to since I had been dealing with all of Justin's drama. However, as much fun as we were having, I have to admit that Justin was on my mind the whole day. I tried my best to block him out.

Justin's phone calls began to come more frequently, and I could feel his anxiousness growing as I kept sending his calls directly to voicemail. When Sierra and I made it back home later that evening from our day of fun, two bouquets of long-stemmed white roses with one red rose in the middle had been delivered to my parents' house with an attached card. Needless to say, I spoke with him on the phone later that night. He was sweet. He was charming. He apologized for our last conversation, and I reluctantly accepted his apology.

three

Show & Prove

My dad came into my room. "What's up?" he asked.

"With what, Daddy?" I answered.

"For months, your mother and I watched you put your life on hold while Justin was locked up. Is this the life that your mother and I worked so hard to see you settle for?" he inquired with concern in his voice.

"No, Dad, but the heart wants what the heart wants," I responded. My father knew that I was a hopeless romantic and that I wanted a fairytale ending, despite the rocky beginning of my relationship with Justin. "Dad, isn't that what you and Mommy had? Huh?"

"Yes, we did," he replied, "but your mother and I were on the same level. We tried our best to shelter you from certain things, but it appears that you are running straight into that lifestyle. I am only telling you this because I love you, and I want you to open your eyes and make the right decision for you and my granddaughter." He gave me a hug and a kiss and said, "Your mom and I will always be here for you. Just always remember that." With that, he left my room.

My dad was right, and his words got me thinking. *I am about to be 31 soon. I'm still living at home with my parents. I have a good job, but I have foolishly been helping Justin out since he's been home.*

This line of thinking necessitated a conversation; I had some serious questions, and I needed some concrete answers. I picked up the phone and dialed Justin's number.

"Babe, what are your intentions for me? For us?" I asked.

"That's easy, Love. I want to make you my wife!"

I smiled. "Okay, well how do you plan on making that happen?"

"Already on it, Babe," he replied confidently.

"What do you mean?" I asked. My curiosity was aroused.

"I wanted to surprise you later at dinner," he said.

"Dinner? When were we going to dinner?" I asked.

"Tonight. I have an announcement to make, and I will make it then. Look pretty for me, okay?"

"Okay!" I answered excitedly. I hung up the phone and raced to the mall; I wanted to be cute for dinner that night, so I needed a new outfit. Surely, I didn't think that Justin was going to propose to me, but I was pleasantly nervous about hearing whatever announcement he was going to make.

We went to one of our favorite seafood restaurants in the marina. Dinner was delicious and the atmosphere relaxing. After my second glass of wine, Justin could clearly see that I was super relaxed and content.

"Babe," he began, "have you wondered why in the last two weeks I have been unavailable?"

"Yes," I responded, trying not to give him that attitude look that I tried my best to camouflage.

He laughed and said, "It was a matter of time. I was running out of excuses!"

"So, what were you doing?" I asked.

"I've been working for a temp agency. I got a great gig in construction," he explained.

"So, why did you hide that from me?" I asked, annoyance in my voice. It seemed strange to me to hide something like that.

"Well, if you let me finish without interrupting me," he said. I quickly apologized, recognizing that I actually had been rudely interrupting him.

He continued, "They hired me on full time! Benefits and all! I got a raise as well. My intention, Love, is to save up for a ring. I want to marry you. I can say that you won't know when I am going to propose, but just know that I am. You are the woman of my dreams, and I plan to grow old with you."

I was beaming! Now, I could take this conversation back to my parents and say, "Boom, Daddy! See? Just because we're not cut from the same cloth does not mean we can't build and grow together!"

Reflecting with happiness on Justin's breaking news, I thought to myself, *This has to be heaven sent. The same day that my father comes to me with his reservations about my man, Justin tells me I'm going to be his wife.* I took the whole thing as assurance that God had made a way to bless our union... or so I thought.

I ran home and burst into my parents' room, eager to share the great news with them. However, after telling them about Justin's new job and the intentions he said he had towards me, they did not share my excitement.

They both looked at me and said, "Consistency is key. Great, he has a job for two weeks. Come back and let us know if he is still employed three years from now."

Disheartened by their response, I told my parents they were just naysayers and too uppity.

My mother responded, "The problem may be, my love, that you are too easy." I exited my parents room feeling irritated.

I remember the next incident that occurred as if it was yesterday. It was a Saturday evening, two months after Justin and I had gone to dinner at the marina. Justin told me that he was going to hang out with his boys.

"Cool, have fun," I said.

At this point, Justin's parents and I were very comfortable with one another. His mother affectionately called me her daughter, and because they loved my company, they even allowed me to spend some weekends at their house with Justin. Thus, it was not strange for me to be asleep in Justin's room if he wasn't there.

This particular Saturday night, Justin was extra-hyper but super-affectionate with me before he left. I told him to be sure and wake me up when he returned home so that he and I could spend some time together. He said, "Absolutely."

Around 2 a.m., I heard Justin entering his room. He was breathing more heavily than usual. He kneeled down by the side of the bed where I lay and gave me a kiss on the cheek, trying to wake me up. Then, he put his hands under the cover fishing for my left hand. When he found it, he kissed my hand, and in the dark, he slowly placed a ring on my ring finger.

He said in the most sincere voice, "I love you with everything I have. Please do me the honor of being your husband."

It had all happened so quickly that I thought I was dreaming! I popped up without even looking at the ring, and in a burst of tears, I cried, "Yes! Yes, Yes!"

We embraced for what seemed like forever. There in his arms, Justin had solidified my existence. No more would I be a single mother, baby mama, girlfriend, or a woman in her thirties who was unmarried and not engaged. I had finally made it! This was the best day *ever*!

Minutes later, I excitedly picked up the phone and called my parents, shouting out the good news to them as soon as they answered.

My father's response, did not match my excitement, to say the least. He simply said, "Congrats," in a monotone voice and advised that I call him in the morning. I thought to myself, *My dad is a trip, but I will show him that I am grown and capable of making my own decisions.*

My mom was still asleep. I guess my father had concluded that my engagement was not a big enough deal to wake my mother. *Are you kidding me?* I kept thinking to myself. I never mentioned my disappointment about my dad's reaction to my fiancé.

four

I Do!

The morning after Justin's proposal, I excitedly opened my eyes to confirm that I was not dreaming! I looked down at my ring finger, and there it was: my beautiful engagement ring! I smiled and rolled over to find him still fast asleep. He looked so peaceful. *My fiancé!* I thought, joy filling my senses. I ran my index finger across his bottom lip and leaned over to kiss him. He woke up.

"Good morning, wifey-to-be!" he said. Those words were music to my ears. My smile grew even bigger.

After we lay in bed for a few minutes discussing the highlights of the previous night's proposal, I remembered that my dad had wanted me to call him. At the same time, however, I also recalled his lackluster reaction to our engagement. Remembrance of this caused my attitude to adjust a bit and wiped away an inch or two from my smile.

Picking up on my body language, Justin asked, "Are you okay, Babe?"

"Yes," I replied. "Why do you ask?"

"Nothing. It just seemed like your vibe changed a bit," he said. I reassured him that he was mistaken, and I quickly changed the subject back to a happy one: our pending nuptials.

I asked, "How long would you like to be engaged?"

"The sooner I can make you my wife, the better," he said. I began to blush.

"Seriously though, Babe, what timeframe were you thinking?" I asked.

"I don't know, maybe three months?" he answered. I shot *that* suggestion down, right off the bat.

"Three months?" I said, echoing his words sarcastically. "Uhhhh, no bueno!" I said. I kindly reminded him that I was planning a wedding, not a barbecue!

Justin laughed and said, "Okay, Babe, what time do you suggest?"

"Let's plan for a year from now," I said.

"No, that's too long! I don't want a year's engagement," Justin replied.

I was feeling a little cocky. I was thinking, *A lot of girls can only get their guy to marry them if they get pregnant, but hell, I got the ring and Justin's intent to marry without a baby!* My esteem was so low at the time that the idea that a man wanted to marry me without the obligation of a baby made me feel like I was on top of the world! I was also thinking, *He can't even wait a whole year to marry me, so he must want me as his wife pretty badly!* In this moment, I felt like I was really winning.

"Okay. I can do six months," I conceded. Justin agreed! I thought to myself, *Look at us compromising already! We are going to be great at this marriage stuff!*

I had asked Justin for a timeframe not only for my own peace, but because it was extremely important that I had answers to some of the questions my parents might ask prior to going home to meet with them. This was especially a concern based on my father's initial reaction to the news the previous night. I was confident that he had some negative feelings about my engagement, so the next time I discussed the matter with him, I wanted to be prepared. I wanted it to appear as if Justin and I had seriously talked things through. One of my parents' biggest pet peeves is when one of their kids has not taken the time to analyze and think through all aspects of a life changing decision, especially one of this magnitude!

Needless to say, I was not looking forward to having this meeting with my parents. However, it was something that I had to do. I made sure that I went by myself.

Before I headed to my parents' house, I called my besties Mia and Scharae. We usually talk for at least a few minutes daily on our way to work. Years ago, we playfully named our conversations the "conference call." That day, on the conference call, I couldn't contain my happiness any longer.

I blurted out, "Justin proposed last night!" followed by a long, deafening scream.

Scharae said, "Awww, congrats sister."

Mia, on the other hand, said "Uhhh, I *know* I told you a long time ago that he is *not right* for you!"

I literally wanted to board a plane to Texas just to wring her neck! How dare she ruin my good news with such a negative statement?

"Not today, devil!" I yelled back at her, and we all started to laugh.

However, she continued. "Sis, my honest truth is that I believe he is not your right match. But you are grown, and you are going to make your own decision. I would just like to go on record with what I said."

"Whatever!" I said. "Our love is different!"

"Okay. I won't be a Debbie Downer. I love you and will rock with you either way. I just want you to be sure you're making the right decision," Mia explained.

I agreed. I *was* grown, and it *was* my decision. I replied in a stern voice, "You are correct. It is my decision. And I believe I am making the right one for me."

Scharae, who felt the tension mounting between Mia and me, chimed in and said, "We are sisters, and we only wish you the best!" I smiled, feeling myself calming down.

"Thank you," I said. "I want you guys to try and be open and give him the benefit of the doubt. Since he's been home, he has handled his business, held down a job and been able to save for an engagement ring for me, making our relationship the priority." They both agreed with what I'd said.

After that, we said our goodbyes, and I headed to my parents' house to once again defend my relationship.

When I walked into the house, I immediately smelled the delicious aroma of my mother preparing a home-cooked traditional Jamaican breakfast in the kitchen. Both of my parents were in the kitchen; my mother was at the stove and my father sat at the kitchen table.

Happy to see my parents and trying to keep a positive spirit, I very cheerfully said, "Good morning, Mom and Dad!"

Mom responded first with a smile. "Morning, mama," she said, affectionately calling me by the nickname she used for me.

"Good morning, baby girl," replied my dad.

Before I could even extend my left hand to show off my engagement ring to my mother, she hastily said, "So, I hear you have some pretty big news to tell me!"

"I sure do!" I said. It was apparent that she didn't know yet. I looked towards my father with a confused look. *Why hadn't he told my mother himself?* I wondered. He looked back at me, waving his hand towards me as if to say, *Go ahead. The floor is all yours.*

I extended my ring finger for my mother to see, and said, "Justin proposed to me last night!" My mother's anxious look turned into a look of concern.

"He did?" she asked. "Well, this indeed is really big news, huh?" She looked in my father's direction with a *Why didn't you tell me this first?* expression.

"Yes!" I exclaimed matter-of-factly. Then, I chose to address the elephant in the room. "It's mighty funny that since I told both you and Dad the news, no one has said 'Congratulations'!"

"I think I can speak for your father as well," my mother responded. "Justin is a nice guy, and we know you two care a great deal for one another, but what is the rush? Marriage is a huge step, and didn't he recently come out of prison?"

"Yes, he did," I said.

My father, who is more cutthroat, began to ask me the hard, confrontational questions.

"How many times has he been locked up? And for what?" He waited for me to answer.

My heart dropped. I knew that I would possibly have to defend Justin against my parents thinking we were moving too fast or not knowing how serious marriage was, but not this! Not the nitty gritty of Justin's personal and dark past.

To answer my father's questions would require me knowing more than the little information that I possessed.

The truth was, all I knew was that Justin had gone to jail the first time on some domestic issues, which he never went into detail about, and he had gone to jail this last time on accusations of being a Peeping Tom. I didn't have any other details, because Justin had never shared any other information with me about the issues. As a matter of fact, Justin did everything in his power *not* to discuss these matters with me in detail. However, there was no way in hell that I would I say any of this to my parents.

I know my parents very well. The pure fact that Justin had been incarcerated at all was enough to completely turn them off of him. Period. If they knew that he was still on parole, they definitely would not care for him at all. Then, there were the details! It would only make matters worse to tell them that Justin had been accused of being a voyeur. This would be the nail in the coffin!

I did what I knew how to do when I found myself in a losing argument with my parents. I deflected, screamed that my parents were being unreasonable, and stormed off crying. I needed a moment away from the double-team of their unified approach. I needed to rethink a new plan and somehow find a way to flip the argument back on my parents, making them defensive instead of me.

I had every intention of still marrying Justin; I just needed my parents to spend some good quality time with him in order to see that yes, he was a bit rough around the edges, but ultimately, he was a really good man. I prayed that in time, they would grow to love him.

Two weeks after the big disagreement with my parents, I made a significant shift in my schedule. I would come home from work, help my daughter with her homework, and then spend time with her. After her dinner and bath, she would go to bed. Then, I would pack my overnight bag and go to my fiancé's parents' house for the night. I returned back to my parents' home every morning so I could take Sierra to school before going to work.

Not surprisingly, my parents did not like this schedule. In fact, I knew that what I was doing was backing them into a corner with me. However, no matter how much they did not approve of the changes I was making, they were aware of a few things. First, I was an adult. Second, I believed that I was in love. Third, they did not want to lose their influence or their relationship with me.

By the third week, my parents were worn down. They came into the room where I was lying down with Sierra, waiting for her to fall asleep before I left to go to Justin's house. My mother started the conversation.

"We love you. You are an adult, and we have instilled morals, integrity and strength in you. This is your journey now, baby. Please remember that you're not on it alone. That little angel that's asleep there is also a part of it, and she should be considered in all you do. So choose wisely. We are not comfortable with this coldness and division that we're feeling, so we will support your wishes. Please just know that if you ever need us, do not let your pride get in the way of coming home."

My father added, "Baby girl, we will always be here for you and Sierra."

With tears streaming down my face, I thought to myself, *The fight is over*. In their own reluctant way, my parents had given me their version of their blessing. This was the best that I was going to get from them, so I took it, no questions asked. I would stay at my parents' house that night and remain there until after the wedding.

My father asked me, "When is the wedding date?"

"In six months," I replied. The look on his face was priceless.

I could tell that my dad wanted to go straight into one of his full rants, but he did not. After all, he didn't want to sound like a total hypocrite after the apology that he and Mom had just given me. My mother also caught my dad's reaction to the timeframe for the wedding. She simply shook her head from side to side, as if to say, "My daughter is an idiot." They left my room.

"Goodnight!" I called out after them as they exited my room. I went straight to sleep that night feeling very contented and victorious. You see, I felt that I had won the battle. Little did I know I would soon be engaged in a full-fledged war!

I threw myself into full wedding planning mode. Planning for the big event seemed to be going pretty smoothly, for the most part. That is, until the morning that I got a phone call from my mother. Her voice sounded weak, as if she had been crying.

"Is everything okay, Mom?" I asked with a voice filled with concern.

She sighed and started to cry. Through her tears, she said, "Your dad had a heart attack this morning."

I immediately started to cry. I asked, "Is he okay?" She didn't know. She said she was at the hospital.

"I'm on my way," I said.

On the way to the hospital, I called Justin. He was very concerned and told me that he would meet me at the hospital. It was comforting to know that I had a fiancé who was so attentive and supportive during difficult times. I felt blessed to know that from now on, I would always have a partner to share life's swift transitions with. God, in His grace, had finally blessed me with my rock.

In the midst of feeling grateful for having Justin there to support me, I couldn't help but wonder, *How would I respond if I had received this news as a single woman?* The thought of receiving such news about my father without Justin being in my life was unbearable.

By this time, in my mind, everything good in my life was associated with Justin. In retrospect, I realize that my intimate relationship with my intended husband was greater than my intimate relationship with my Savior, Jesus Christ. I had foolishly allowed my relationship with Justin to become my priority in life – a greater priority than God, and an even greater priority than my daughter.

God allows us free will: the ability to make our own choices. I freely made the choice that my relationship with Justin was the most important thing in my life, and I treated it as such. God would eventually deal with me Himself directly as it related to my choice.

I reached the hospital and rushed straight to my father's bedside. He was hooked up to all sorts of monitors but was conscious and somewhat alert. It was stressful to see my hero lying there so weak and helpless. This was the man that had always protected, cared for and loved me. Just to be in his presence offered me a calmness because of our bond and love for another. Now, I kind of felt that the tables had been turned. I felt like the protector in this moment rather than the protected.

I leaned in and whispered, "Hi, Daddy. I'm here," while holding his hands. He looked at me and squeezed my hand softly. I smiled. Just that fast, he became my protector again.

His doctor walked into the hospital room and started to explain my father's test results to us. Apparently, Dad had had a semi-serious heart attack. The doctor confirmed that Dad had blocked arteries and that surgery was necessary to clear the blockage. In surgery, they would add a stent to help the blood flow. My dad was scheduled to have the surgery the next morning.

From there, the doctor took the opportunity to explain how my father needed to change his diet and to exercise, and how imperative it was for him to get these things under control. Then, the doctor questioned whether my dad had been under a great deal of pressure or stress lately. There was an awkward silence. I noticed that my father's eyes had shifted in my direction.

At the time, I told myself that it was nothing but a coincidence; my dad had just *happened* to look over at me when the doctor asked him about his stress. I labeled it a coincidence so that I could ignore the intense sadness and grief that threatened to rise up in me if it had not been a coincidence.

The truth was that I didn't want to know the true answer. I could not bear the pain of knowing the truth, if in fact, it was true. What if my father was so heartbroken about my wedding that it caused him to experience a level of stress that could trigger a heart attack? Rather than dwell on the matter, however, I managed to bury the feeling deep down inside.

For the next couple of months after my father's heart attack, the doctor placed him under a strict diet and exercise plan. Justin was very instrumental in assisting and encouraging my dad to stay on track, along with my two nephews. Justin would help prepare some of my father's meals, and my nephews were in charge of making sure that he exercised.

This might seem like a horrible thing to say, but it appeared that the heart attack might have brought my parents and Justin closer. My parents were becoming much more comfortable with him, which made it easier to see that he was a sincerely likeable guy. They both were impressed with how family oriented and respectful he was. He was not the scholar that my parents would have preferred that I marry, but he loved me and my daughter.

As a result of Justin being around more and spending time with my parents, I was feeling more relaxed. Having to always try and sell him to my mother and father as a suitable choice for a partner had been taxing on my energy and my nerves. I was glad that they were slowly coming around. Now, I could save my focus and energy for all of the wedding preparations, which were still underway. We were a couple of months away from MY big day!

The wedding was less than six weeks away. I was now in my "finalize" period. Dress, check. Location, check. Flowers, check. Invitations, check. Bridesmaids' dresses and groomsmen's tuxes, check!

We were having a traditional church wedding. A few months prior, Justin had joined a local community church and invited me and Sierra to attend it with him. We did, and we instantly fell in love with the congregation. Not to mention that the church had a beautiful sanctuary. Now that Justin was a member of the church, we were able to be married there.

I thought that having our wedding at Justin's new church would be an easy process; we would give them the date, they would charge us a fee, we would pay it, and we would hold our wedding there. However, it was nowhere near that easy.

The pastor at the church was very traditional. In order to use the church and for him to preside at our wedding, he required us to complete his six-week marriage counseling sessions. In these sessions, he would explain what it truly meant, biblically, to enter in a marriage union as a Christian and what God says about marriage. In retrospect, Justin and I must have both been in a deep coma while we went through the sessions. Even though the pastor was very detailed about what marriage means when you enter it as a Christian and what is expected from you in the partnership, both individually and as a couple, we were just going through the motions. If we had really been mature and solid in our relationship we would have, and should have, discussed in more detail what we learned, and what we felt about what was being taught to us. More importantly, we would have had a greater focus on what God says about marriage!

We didn't. We were so wrapped up in the idea of getting married and celebrating our big day together, that rather than getting prepared to share our LIFE walk as partners forever, we simply prepared for the celebration. One day of celebration trumped our life partnership. In layman's terms, the wedding was bigger than the marriage.

Ideally, the six weeks that we spent in the counseling sessions would have been the opportune time to confess that this step that we were about to make was bigger than us, and that truthfully, we were not ready. We could have made the decision to not marry right away, postponing the wedding. We could have taken some time to figure some things out before we made a big mess.

I can also honestly say that at that moment, I didn't have any doubts in my mind. You see, I had mastered how to tuck away my questions and concerns about what had happened earlier in our relationship. I was no longer in defense mode; I was in full-steam ahead mode! After all, Justin and I had already had so much invested in getting married. Besides, who calls off a wedding a week or two before the big day? Not me! Heck, I had family flying in and everything. Too much was at stake.

❧

It was a week before the wedding, and everything was moving at warp speed. All of my brothers were flying in this week; my two older brothers from my mother were coming with their families, and my father's son was coming too. They wanted to have a proper introduction to my husband-to-be before the festivities. I was super nervous about my older brothers meeting him, especially my biological brothers. They had been witnesses to my mother's abuse by my biological father, so they would be very protective of their little sister with whomever I decided to marry in order to ensure that the same didn't happen to me.

My brothers were professional men; they did very well for themselves financially. The eldest is a CEO and founder of a headhunting company. My other older brother is the executive district manager for a Fortune 500 company. To say that they are overprotective would be an understatement as it pertains to my brothers' relationship with me. I was their baby and the only girl.

My parents had planned a formal dinner for when my brothers came into town so that they could be formally introduced to Justin. We weren't even an hour into the dinner before I could tell that both of my older brothers had already made up their minds that Justin was not the right fit for me. They were not rude or insulting, but they did, in my opinion, come off as uninviting and sort of standoffish. However, what I respected and loved about my fiancé was that he was his own man; he never needed, or was bothered by, people's opinions of him. I always admired that confidence he exuded.

Justin made it painfully clear at the dinner table that he was entering into marriage with me and Sierra, and we were the only two people whose opinions mattered.

"Duly noted!" my eldest brother responded. "She is our baby sister, and my niece will always be our main concern." That dinner couldn't have ended any quicker for me.

On the morning of the wedding rehearsal, I called Scharae, my maid of honor, regarding some last minute wedding to do's. She sounded somber, so I asked her what was up. She mentioned that she was going through something but did not want to get into it, as we were on the eve of my big day.

She quickly shifted the conversation and asked if we should call Mia, because there was a big storm brewing in Louisiana. Mia resides in Texas in a city only a few hours away from Louisiana, so Scharae was concerned. I agreed. We got Mia on the line for our "conference call."

Initially, Mia was in the wedding party. However, she had found out a few weeks prior that she and her husband were expecting their third child. We were ecstatic for her and relieved to hear that her illness, which we had been discussing on our conference call before knowing she was pregnant, was a blessing and not something serious. Unfortunately, though, she wasn't going to be able to make it to the wedding.

We got Mia on the call and talked about the progress of the impending storm. As it turned out, the storm that was brewing was Hurricane Katrina. Thus, on that day, Scharae was in her own personal storm and Mia also had her own storm on the horizon. Little did I know that I was walking into a 10-year storm myself.

The wedding rehearsal went off without a hitch. Justin was a bit irritated due to his kids' mother threatening that she would not allow his son and daughter to attend our wedding. He told me he was going to the kids' house to try and talk some sense into his ex-girlfriend with hopes of convincing her to allow his kids to be a part of the wedding.

We had planned for Justin's son to be the ring bearer and his daughter to be a flower girl alongside my daughter, Sierra. As he left, I warned him not to get into a long fight with his ex-girlfriend over the matter. He promised me that he wouldn't.

"Goodnight," I said to my husband-to-be.

"I will see you at the altar," he replied. He kissed me slowly and passionately. I was the luckiest girl in the world... or so I thought.

The next morning, I woke up with great excitement. *Today is my wedding day!* I thought to myself. I was the happiest woman in the world. Scharae's voice, my maid of honor, was the first voice I heard.

"Good morning, bride!" she said jubilantly.

"Hey girl! What's up?" I responded eagerly.

"Listen, there's a lot to do and in a little timeframe," she said.

"I know, right?" I replied.

"I am on my way to pick up Sierra. I already have Justin's daughter with me."

"Really? How did you get her?" I asked.

"Too much drama to get into, but she is with me, and Justin has his son. The groomsmen are already on their way to the barbershop. You need to head to your suite so your hair stylist and makeup artist can start on you," she instructed.

I let out a sigh of relief. I know she said there had been some drama about Justin's kids, but the good news was that he had his son, and Scharae had his daughter. *Whew, dodged a bullet there! My wedding will not be ruined.* I thought. That was all that mattered to me at that moment. I had worked too hard to put the wedding together and did not want it to be spoiled on my wedding day. Even if I had wanted all of the gory details, Scharae would not have gone into them. She would not allow distractions to cross my path. Not on her watch!

When I got up to check on Sierra, she was already having breakfast.

"Good morning, Mommy!"

"Good morning, Love Bug!" I responded. My dad had prepared for me a wonderful light breakfast with delicious fruits and pastries. I sat next to Sierra, glowing.

I whispered in her ear, "You know, after today a lot of things are going to change for the better for us."

She nodded her head in agreement and whispered back to me, "I know you really want to be married, Mommy. I am happy for you." Then she asked, "Will you still always love me?"

"Nothing in the world can make me stop loving you! I want you to know that," I said. Sierra smiled and nodded her head. I gave her a kiss and told her that her godmother was on her way with her new stepsister so they could go get their hair done. I would see her at the church before the wedding.

Sierra gave me the biggest hug, as if she didn't want to let me go, and said, "See you soon, Mommy."

What Sierra never communicated to me was that she really never liked Justin. She loved me and knew how badly I wanted to be married. Looking back, I realized that I never really asked Sierra how she felt about Justin. In my mind, I was the adult, so I didn't owe anyone any explanations or have to seek any permission about what I did. I never wanted to answer questions about why we had to go the parole station or whether what the lady at the parole office had said about Justin was true. It's not like I had many answers anyway, because Justin never actually gave me any clear answers about the accusations against him.

Scharae and my stepdaughter made it to my house. The girls were excited to have a day of being pampered. They were getting a manicure, a pedicure, and their hair done, and they were putting on pretty dresses. I said my goodbyes to my daughters and Scharae. Then, my mother and I jumped into her car. She and I were on our way to check into my hotel where my hairstylist and makeup artist was going to make us look flawless!

Hours away from my big wedding, my bestie, Mia, called me.

"Hey, girl!" I said enthusiastically.

"Hey, girly!" she said. "Well, today is the big day, huh?"

"It sure is!" I could tell she was trying to pick her words carefully. She was trying not to upset me on my wedding day.

"Sister, marriage is hard, and it pulls from you daily. I want you to be up for the challenge. Your wedding day is completely different than the actual marriage."

I interrupted her. "Not today, Mia."

"I'm not trying to be a Debbie Downer. I just want you to go into it fully equipped. And know that no matter what, I love you, and I will always be there for you, okay?"

"Okay. Thanks," I said. "How are you feeling with the baby and all?"

"I'm okay. Just a bit sick. Nothing major. But what I am *more* worried about is Hurricane Katrina." She and her family were in a hotel, as the storm has caused her house to flood a bit. We both had a major laugh about how the outspoken rapper, Kanye West, had spoken his truth about President Bush concerning his treatment of the people affected by Hurricane Katrina. West's controversial comments had made the national news. After our chuckle, I told her that I would call her when we were on our honeymoon.

"My husband and I," I said in a very boastful tone, "are flying off to Orlando, Florida for a week to a resort hotel, compliments of my parents. Say a prayer for us, please?"

"Will do," Mia said. "Talk to you soon." I told her I loved her, and I thanked her for not going on about my man, at least not today.

"No worries," she responded. "I have plenty of time to speak my truth, just not today."

I agreed, saying, "Yes, just not today."

My hairstylist finished my mother's hair and told me to wrap up the call, because I was next.

"I need to go. I'm about to be primped!" I said. I told her that I would talk with her later. As I made my way to the stylist's chair, I looked at my mother's hair; it was flawless. She made her way to my makeup artist's section in the suite to get started as my stylist began to do my hair.

I was a ball of nerves. I wanted so badly to talk with Justin. On a normal day, he and I would have already talked with each other at least five times by now. However, we were trying to do the "see you at the altar" deal where we couldn't talk with each other until we were ready to say "I do!"

I am also happy to say that since Justin and I had been in marriage counseling for six weeks, we had not been sexually active. That was the hardest resolution that we had decided upon in our relationship. Actually, wait… let me be *real*: this was the hardest rule that *I* implemented and that *he* had to go along with!

I knew that I wasn't a pure bride. Hell, I had a nine-year-old kid! But I wanted to be as close to a virgin as I could be before I said my vows. I was proud that we did not break the rules, although we had had some close calls over the past six weeks. However, we never broke our promise. Therefore, I was looking forward to tonight – on *every* level. I would get to make love to my *husband*! This time, when I made love to Justin, it would be beautiful in the eyes of the Lord because of our new union.

My hair was pinned up in big, beautiful curls with curly strands dangling on the nape of my neck. My stylist had placed the veil on my head. Now, for the first time, I felt like a bride. At this point, I only had on my veil. I would put my wedding dress on at the church. My makeup was also stunning. I couldn't believe how beautiful I looked! When I came out of the bedroom, my mother began to cry.

"Mom, please do not cry off your makeup. That would send me over the top," I said to her in the most loving tone.

My mother smiled and nodded her head as if to agree with me. I asked the makeup artist to retouch my mother's makeup. I was so grateful to be able to spend this bonding moment with my mother. I could still see the hint of concern on my mother's face, but she did her best to mask it in fear that I would pick up on her emotions.

It was time to make our way to the church. Before I left the hotel room, I laid out on the bed the lingerie that my stylist had bought for me as a wedding gift. This was the same hotel room that my husband and I would return to after our big celebration.

As we were on our way down to the lobby, my bestie and maid of honor, Scharae, called to check on us.

"Perfect timing, Sis!" I said cheerfully.

"What are we doing now?" she asked.

"We're on our way out of the hotel and headed to the church," I answered.

"Are you in the lobby?" she asked.

"Yes, why?" I replied.

"Walk out of the front door," she said.

"I am. What's going on?" I was getting anxious.

"You will see!" she said. In front of the hotel was a black-on-black 745 BMW with a driver.

"Ma'am, your car awaits you!" Scharae said excitedly. I was so happy! That was my favorite car, and my fiancé made sure that I arrived in style for our wedding!

"What? I can't believe it!" I exclaimed. She could hear the excitement in my voice.

"My part is done!" she said.

Scharae had been the only one communicating with Justin on my wedding day, and this was a surprise set-up by him for me. I can honestly say that I felt like a queen on that day. My mother and I got into the car and headed to the church where I would see my daughters all dressed up and ready to go.

Pulling up to the church, I could feel the butterflies fluttering around my stomach. I wasn't worried about the actual ceremony or the commitment of marriage; I was more nervous about the event. I had worked so hard on getting things in order, and I didn't want anything to go wrong on this day. You can clearly see that my priorities were not in order.

I made my way to the holding area for the bridal party. In my quarters, my bridesmaids and my daughters were waiting. My mother and I walked into the room. There was a gasp, and my girlfriends cried in unison, "Awww, you look *so* pretty!" I chuckled.

Sierra ran up to me and gave me a big hug. After her day of primping and preparing for the wedding, I could tell that she had missed my presence and was a bit anxious. She looked so pretty, all dolled-up. I then directed my attention to my new daughter-to-be and began to compliment her on how pretty she looked as well. I had to be careful to learn how to spread out my attention between the kids. Even though Justin's kids would not officially be living with us after we were married, I wanted to be sure that they felt included, as we were now a blended family. I did not want anyone to feel less special or important than anyone else. I loved all my kids, and I wanted them to sincerely feel it.

Scharae began to update me, letting me know that everything was on target and that Justin had arrived at the church with his groomsmen. I was relieved to know that my husband-to-be was under the same roof as me and getting ready for our nuptials. I wanted so badly to call him just to hear his voice, but I was determined to stick to our resolve to not communicate at all with one another until we saw each other at the altar.

We were now about an hour away from the wedding. I had slipped into my wedding dress, and suddenly, it all felt surreal. "I am about to be a wife!" I said. *Woah! I had said it out loud. A wife!* The title alone made me glow. I felt validated, like I was now about to be a part of a prestigious group. Someone had loved me enough to ask for my hand in marriage. This was the validation that I so longed for, and today my dreams would come true.

Standing around with my bridesmaids in the bridal suite, I remember taking a moment to say a heartfelt "Thank you" and "I love you" to each one of my bridesmaids before we left for the sanctuary. I had three bridesmaids: Mo, who was my friend that had attended Justin's 30th birthday party with me; Justin's favorite female cousin, Courtney, whom I hit it off with when we were first introduced to each other; and Stacy, Scharae's cousin, whom I've always adored. Stacy graciously stood in for Mia, who was in Texas dealing with the illness of a new pregnancy and the effects of a hurricane. Luckily, Stacy and Mia were the same size, so she was able to fit into Mia's dress. Last but not least, Scharae was my maid of honor, my "ride or die." She was the glue that held me together that day.

Before my makeup had a chance to run due to all of my sappy emotions, there was a knock at the door. It was my daddy. He looked so handsome in his tux! His reaction when he saw me in my gown was adorable. I think I actually saw him fight back a tear that was attempting to fall.

"You are beautiful! Simply stunning, Baby Girl!" he told me. I allowed my tears to drop. My father was my hero. Any compliment that he gave me was sincere and genuine, and his love for me is true. I gave him a huge hug.

"Can we have a few minutes alone?" he whispered.

"Certainly," I responded. I asked the ladies if they would excuse us for a moment.

"Perfect timing," Scharae said, as it was time for the flower girls and bridesmaids to line up for their entry.

My dad reached for my left hand, kissed it, and said, "It's not too late!" He said it in a joking manner, but for some strange reason, I detected a bit of truth in his humor.

"Daddy, quit playing!" I said.

"Okay. Just remember, Love, I am always here for you and Sierra. Whenever you need us, your mother and I will be here for you, no questions asked. Promise me you will always remember that?" he said, looking into my eyes.

"I promise," I said.

"Okay. Let's get this show on the road! You have a very lucky man that gets the honor of calling you his wife!" he said as he led me towards the door to exit the bridal suite.

I kissed my dad, and he and I waited for my wedding song to play before I walked into the sanctuary to finally become a Mrs.!

Our wedding was beautiful. When we said our vows to one another, I was serious and very much in the moment. I meant every word that I spoke. I loved this man with all my heart, and I believed that he loved me the same way.

After the wedding, we took pictures at the church with our parents and the bridal party. Our guests made their way to our garden reception, which was to be hosted by my uncle at his house. Talk about having a good time at the reception! Justin and I and our guests had a ball. They especially loved the all-night open bar, compliments of my father and brothers.

At the end of our festive day of celebration, Justin and I were both tired. Around 1 a.m., I expressed to Justin that I was super tired, and I was ready to go back to the hotel. He told me that he was exhausted as well.

"Let's go home, Wife," he said. I gave him a sexy little smile, like, *Yes!* That was who I was, Justin's wife! We said goodnight to the remaining guests and made our way to the car, where our driver had been waiting for us patiently.

When we made it back to my room, we both were exhausted. We wanted to make love to each other; after all, we had not been intimate with each other since before we started to attend our marriage counseling classes with our pastor. However, after I fought to take off my makeup, veil, wedding dress and remove all the bobby pins from my hair, a process that felt like another two whole hours to successfully complete, I was completely worn out. We both were.

We climbed into the bed, and my husband kissed me so slowly and softly.

"Goodnight, Baby," I said.

"Goodnight, Love," he whispered back.

"Get a lot of rest tonight. We have a lot to make up for in the morning!"

He nodded his head and said, "Alright, Babe." We both closed our eyes and drifted off to sleep.

five

Home Sweet Home

Our first morning as man and wife was absolutely beautiful. We made love, and our connection was *amazing*! We laid in bed feeling excited about our honeymoon in Florida, which we would be leaving for the next morning. However, first, we had some errands to run before our departure, and we also wanted to spend some time with our kids. There was a lot to do, so we got up and started our day.

To me, officially being married felt different. I know that a lot of people say that the only difference between being married and unmarried is simply a piece of paper that legally ties you to someone. However, in my case, I actually felt different. I felt happier. I felt *valued*.

Justin and I completed all of our errands, and then we picked up our kids and spent the day with them. We wanted to spend as much time with them as possible before departing for our honeymoon the next morning. We were only going to be gone for a week, but I was having some separation anxiety.

I had never been away from Sierra that long. I knew she was going to be just fine; she was staying with her grandparents, who completely and endlessly spoil her.

Justin and I made it to the airport early the next morning to board our flight. We both were very excited to spend a week together by ourselves and enjoy some uninterrupted time. We hadn't had a chance to talk with each other about the highlights of our wedding yet, as we had been on the move since our wedding day.

"We have a lot to discuss," he said, "like when are we going to move into our own place?" He was adamant that we make the move once we returned from our honeymoon.

I agreed and said, "We will look into it as soon as we get back."

The flight was great. Still exhausted, we slept just about the entire plane ride. After we landed in Florida, we made it to the hotel and discovered that my parents had booked us a luxury suite, all inclusive! The honeymoon suite was breathtaking. Our first night in Florida, we didn't leave the hotel room. It felt good to make love to my husband and know that we were not sinning against God. I felt liberated.

The next morning when I woke up, Justin was not in the bed with me. I got up and checked the bathroom. There was no sign of him. I noticed that the door of our bedroom, which led into the living area of the suite, was open. I walked out into the living area to see if Justin was in the room, but he was not there, either. Just then, I heard a muffled sound.

Our suite also had an adjoining room to which we had access, but we hadn't spent any time in it because only the two of us were there. Drawing closer to the door of the room, I could now hear the strong sound of Justin's voice. It sounded like he was on the phone. He was talking loudly, as if he was irritated. I put my ear to the door in an attempt to try to make out his words. Clearly, he was talking to his kids' mother.

I couldn't believe it! *Wait? What?* I thought, as I felt my anger growing. *I know he is not speaking to his kids' mother on our honeymoon!* I yanked the door open. His back was turned toward me, and he didn't notice that I was in the room with him while he was yelling.

I was fuming. "Justin!"

He turned around, shocked that I was in the room.

"Hey Babe, this girl is *tripping*!" He said, hanging up the phone.

"Why are you on the phone with her on our honeymoon?" I asked accusingly. "Better yet, why did you come in this room to speak with her? Why are you allowing anyone to set you off when this trip is about us?"

I gave him no room to respond. I could not care less about his answers. The questions were rhetorical. No response that he could possibly try to use as a defense would have worked. In fact, I prayed that he would recognize by the inflection in my voice and expression on my face that he should not even *try* to answer.

Clearly, Justin didn't notice, because he went straight into trying to answer my rhetorical questions. He tried to explain that he was calling his kids, because he hadn't spoken to them since we had seen them after the wedding. He wanted to see if they were okay. When he felt that his answers weren't working, he tried to turn the argument on me.

"We are on our *honeymoon*!" I reminded him sharply. "I haven't even checked on Sierra yet, because I left her in great hands!" I could understand if we had been in Florida a few days and hadn't spoken to our kids, but we had only been there for one night! *Something's not right*, my gut told me.

"Heck," I continued, "you were gone for eight months when you were locked up, and I know you missed your kids desperately then, too, but you didn't check on them every day. It's not like they aren't accustomed to you leaving for lengthy amounts of time without a daily conversation. So what's a week?"

Justin told me that I was overreacting and being childish.

"Okay," I said. "So let's not get off topic. If you were calling to talk to your kids, how did you and she get into an argument?"

Once again, he flashed me the same deer-in-the-headlights stare he always had when he got caught. In my mind, I thought, *I pray that he finds another look to display when he gets caught off guard. I can't take this look for the rest of our lives.*

He stuttered a bit and said, "She was mad at me that we got married."

"Okay, but why are you arguing? It sounded to me like she told you how she felt, which she is entitled to. But why do you have anger? What is there to be angry about?"

"There you go, Bree. Always trying to make an issue more than what it is," he responded.

"Justin, I'm not trying to do any such thing. If you can explain to me why you got so mad, and why you took time away from our honeymoon to talk with her, then I will listen. Babe, who gets into an argument on their *honeymoon*? Let's stop and refocus on us."

"I'm sorry about that. I didn't want to disturb you when you were sleeping, so I came into this room. I love you, and I don't want to fight with my wife," he said sweetly.

I agreed to drop it because I didn't want to argue with my husband about another woman – especially not on my honeymoon. However, I made a mental note to myself: *It seems like there is some unfinished business between the two of them.* My gut told me to pay attention.

I tried my best to not let that incident ruin our whole trip. We actually had a blast the remainder of our time in Florida. We ended up going out after a few days in the hotel room, of course, venturing out to the tourist spots and restaurants, and doing lots of shopping. We made sure we brought back plenty of gifts for our kids. We also made sure that we didn't visit Disney World; we wanted to take that trip with the kids in the near future.

After our honeymoon week ended, we headed home, back to my parents' house. We had a lot of planning to do. We needed to find our own place to live within 30 days, because Justin did not want to be in my parents' home any longer than that.

Once we got settled, we started the apartment shopping process immediately. Three weeks later, we found an apartment that we liked. The beauty of it was that it was in the same city as my parents, which meant that Sierra didn't have to change schools.

The stress of apartment shopping must have worn me down. Between work, caring for Sierra, and being a newlywed, I became run down and felt under the weather frequently. I thought I had come down with the stomach flu. Due to my sickness, I missed a week of work, which was not good, as I had taken a lot of time off while planning the wedding and being away for my honeymoon.

I went to the doctor to see if he could offer me any relief from my flu-like symptoms. My doctor drew a blood sample and discovered that I was four weeks pregnant. I was stunned. He ordered me to take off work for the next month, because I was classified as a high-risk pregnancy due to my miscarriage in the past.

I called Justin as soon as I left the doctor's office. He was so happy! He laughed out loud and said, "I told you that first night in Florida that you were pregnant when we finished making love!"

"Heck, I guess you were right!" I replied.

This was coming at a great time for our new family. We were scheduled to move into our new apartment in a week, and now, we knew why I had been feeling so under the weather. This was such a different feeling from my last pregnancy, the one that I had kept hidden from my parents when Justin and I first began dating.

I ran home and told my parents our news. They were very excited for us and offered us their congratulations. Sierra was also very happy to hear that she was going to be a big sister and not an only child anymore. Things were finally looking up for my new family!

Moving day finally came. The day was long and a bit stressful. I was no help in the moving process, because I was extremely sick from the pregnancy. The term "morning sickness" should be changed to "all day sickness" as it related to me. However, we managed to get everything moved into our new place. Our little apartment was quaint, with two bedrooms and a bathroom. It was a small, starter place, the first step in a building process for our little family, but it was our home.

Justin and I had a circle of friends that were all couples, and we hung out with our friends all the time. We would take trips together, celebrate birthdays, have barbeques, and enjoy couples' nights. You name it, and we all did it together.

I became very close with one of the women in the group. Her name was Roxy, and she was a firecracker, a social butterfly, and an all-around friend. She and I found ourselves breaking away from the couples group at times and having an occasional girls' night out by ourselves. Roxy and I became confidantes down the line. We'd already shared a common thread with each other: she'd grown up with both of my besties, Scharae and Mia back in the day. My besties had also agreed that Roxy was a true blue friend.

Roxy had a little girl who was about a year old when I first met her. I remember that I was so jealous of her, because I would have done anything to have already delivered my bundle of joy. I was about seven months pregnant at the time, and I was miserable. Mia had just delivered my niece, a healthy bundle of joy. I kept trying to cheer myself on by saying, "I'm next!"

Justin and I were now in full preparation mode for our soon-to-arrive bundle of joy. I had been off of work for the majority of my pregnancy due to my being high-risk and having complications throughout the pregnancy. Twice, I had been hospitalized for being dehydrated. I could not keep water down, let alone food.

We came to the easy decision to ask our great friends, Jack and Michelle, who had been married for more than 10 years at the time, to be our baby's godparents. Justin had introduced me to them in the beginning of our relationship. Jack and Justin were good friends. The guys had taken Michelle and I out of town for a weekend, and she and I had hit it off. Michelle is a charismatic, fun loving, and genuine woman, and she is the kind of person who is all about logistics. When we asked her and her husband to do us the honor of being our baby's godparents, they happily accepted. Michelle had been nine months pregnant at the time of our wedding, expecting her first child. Not long after our wedding, she and Jack were blessed with a beautiful baby girl. I was blessed to have such strong connections with new people in my life that I had made through their connection to Justin.

Another connection that I made through Justin was one that I became re-connected to from my past. Earlier in our relationship, Justin told me that he'd had a girl for a best friend, prior to our relationship. Before I met her, I was a bit leery of getting to know her. The first time he brought us together, when we were dating, I was nervous.

All I knew about Justin's female best friend was that her name was Tiff, and she was a hairstylist. We had gone to her shop. When I walked in and saw her, I started to smile. As it turned out, "Tiff," as he called her, was my girl, Tiffany! She used to do my hair back in the day, and I had always been fond of her.

Realizing that we recognized one another, Justin shook his head and said, "Y'all know each other?"

"Yes!" we yelled.

Tiffany started to laugh and said, "Whew! I was wondering who you were going to walk up in here with. I'm so glad it's Bree! You guys make a lovely couple." Tiffany also knew Sierra's father and asked how he was she doing. It felt like a mini reunion.

Whenever Tiffany and Justin were together, it was straight comedy. They fed off of each other, and both of them were crazy! I was so happy to be connected with her again. From that day on, Tiffany became my hairstylist. Hairstylists play an important role in women's lives; they often share a close, comfortable bond and even become like mini-therapists in their clients' lives. Tiffany certainly played that role in my life, especially since she knew both Justin and me well.

Two days after my baby shower, when I was eight months pregnant, Justin and I went on one of our daily walks, as instructed by our doctor for a healthy delivery. As we walked, a stray dog began running towards me. Justin had brought his dog, whom he had named "The General," along for our walk. I had never interacted with his dog, because it lived at his parents' home. I was scared of The General.

When The General saw the stray dog approaching me, he darted in front of me to protect me. However, because I was scared of The General, I did not read his move as protective. The confusion of the stray dog running towards me and The General darting in front of me caused me to trip over Justin's dog, and I fell directly on my stomach. I was knocked out from the shock.

When I woke up, Justin was leaning over me. I put my hand on my stomach, and I couldn't feel our baby kicking anymore. The baby had been active during our walk, and now, there was nothing. We rushed straight to the hospital and were told that the baby was in distress; because of the fall, the baby was now breached. All I could do was cry. I kept thinking *No, God. Please, not again. I am so attached to our baby.* At the time, I didn't know if our baby was a boy or a girl; we had always asked the doctors and nurses not to tell us, because we wanted to be surprised. Now, it seemed like there could be a possibility that I might lose another one of Justin's babies, a son or a daughter. I couldn't bear to go through that pain again.

I had given birth to Sierra naturally with no epidural, so I was expecting to do the same with this baby. However, the doctor came in and said that he had to do a caesarian section because he was concerned about how much pressure the baby might be experiencing. I agreed. I was *scared*, but Justin was there with me every step of the way.

The procedure was a quick one. I felt tugging and pressure, and then out came my beautiful baby girl, whom we named Kennedy. She was perfect! She was premature and only weighed four pounds, but she was a fighter! God had answered my prayers and then some, because within two days of her birth, she was able to go home with us. She passed all her tests and picked up weight, so our doctor was comfortable with releasing her. I now had a Sierra and a Kennedy. Could my life get any better?

Justin was in love with his new daughter. To be clear, he loved all of his kids dearly. However, Kennedy was the first of his children that he had been able to really participate with up close as an active father, from the time she was conceived until her birth. It was an experience that was a lot different than seeing his kids on a weekly basis or every other weekend. To this day, Kennedy and Justin have an unbreakable bond. I am comfortable in saying that I believe she is one of the reasons why he tries his best in all that he does.

When Sierra first held Kennedy, I could see the love and instant protection she felt for her little sister. Sierra was the best big sister! She was gentle, patient and loving.

Things were going well. We were still being newlyweds and settling into the rhythm of being a blended family with a newborn daughter. However, with a new baby, our little apartment started to get cramped and feel a lot smaller. Although I was still officially on a leave of absence from my job, I knew that I didn't want to go back to it; I was no longer happy with the hours required or the distance that I had to commute to and from work.

I shared my thoughts about the job with Justin, explaining to him that I also wanted to make more money and move into a bigger place. He agreed that I should start a job search, so I began to look for a new job while I was still on disability leave.

With the new baby and Sierra, I started to feel a bit overwhelmed. When I tried to talk with Justin about how I felt, I kept feeling that he was becoming distant. *Is it because I've picked up extra weight from the pregnancy?* I wondered. I felt as though my husband was not that attracted to me anymore, and I was getting concerned. My intuition, which I believe every woman has, was kicking into high gear.

First, I started to notice that Justin's cell phone was always on vibrate. When I questioned him about it, he would always have an instant attitude, which only stirred up more questions in my mind. Then, I was at home daily with our kids while he was gone the majority of the day at work. However, after work, he no longer came straight home. Instead, he chose to hang out with his boys after work and come home later.

I did what a majority of women do when we suspect something: I started my investigation. My assistant was the internet. Justin and I shared a mobile phone bill together, so I decided to begin here. *Surely, I will be able to see a pattern of what's going on from the phone records*, I thought. I was right. When I pulled up our phone bills, I saw a lot of unnecessary phone calls to his kids' mother – daily! I immediately had a flashback to our honeymoon when I'd caught him on the phone with her.

In addition to his kids' mother's phone number, there were other unfamiliar phone numbers, which I promptly called. Yes, I called to listen to the gender of the person who answered the phone. Each was a female, and I did not recognize any of their voices. Even if they didn't answer, they did me the favor of having a voicemail recording, which gave me their name, and advised that they were unable to answer the phone. I diligently wrote down all of their names, numbers, and the times and dates of the phone calls. Then, I went to my calendar to match the calls up with the days that they had been made in order to establish a timeline.

As I reviewed the information on the phone bills, what blew me away the most was that our bill for our cell phones had consistently been in the $300-$500 range, each month. I had never known this, because Justin always made sure to pay it promptly.

The discovery that my husband had been secretly talking to other women brought me to an important decision: I knew that it was imperative for me to get back to work ASAP! I needed to get out of my everyday 'bun and sweats' look; it was time to bring back the attractive, polished, professional Bree. If Justin was being lured away by other women because I had 'let myself go,' I was going to get myself together again and regain my husband's attention. However, I was still prepared to confront him with the new information that I had uncovered in my research. I was on a mission. *He is not going to flip the argument on me this time,* I thought. *I have too much information.*

Before I could confront my husband with my findings, the other shoe dropped. Kennedy was about six months old at the time, and she was lying in her playpen in my room. Sierra, now 11 years old, came into my room.

"Hi, Mommy." She had a confused, awkward look on her face.

I said, "What's up, Babe? Are you getting your stuff together to spend the night with your daddy?"

"I already did that," she answered. "I just need you to look it over to make sure I have everything."

"Okay. Go and bring it," I said.

"Mom, I didn't come in here to talk about that," she said.

"Okay. What's on your mind, Babe?" I tried my hardest to act like I was in a good mood, not showing any signs that I was stressed out about my recent findings about the phone bill.

"Do husbands and wives look at each other when they're alone?" she asked uncomfortably.

Huh? I honestly didn't understand the question. "Sierra, what are you talking about?" The next words that fell out of her mouth marked the beginning of my twilight zone.

"When you take showers, Dad watches you. I wanted to know if you knew that, or maybe if that is what married people do?" It literally felt like two uncomfortable minutes went by before I could respond.

"What do you mean, Baby?" I was breathless. Sierra could tell that I was anxious.

"Mommy, there are times when you take a shower and he watches you. At first, I thought maybe it was an accident, but then I noticed that every time you are in the shower, he watches you, and when I come out of the room, he acts like he was doing something or getting something, but he really wasn't," she explained. I was shocked.

"Yes, Mommy knows," I lied. "One day when you get married, you will understand."

Sierra gave me a hug and looked me straight in the eyes like she was trying to look through my soul, as if she knew that I was not telling the truth. She took Kennedy into her room to play and left me sitting on the edge of my bed with a blank stare on my face.

I shook my head back and forth. *This can't be true,* I thought. All I kept seeing were images of the little lady at the parole office. Who would have thought that when I woke up this morning feeling blessed, by the end of the day, I would discover that my husband was possibly cheating on me, and worse, that he was watching me in my private time. I wanted to crawl back into bed and start the day over.

When Justin came home, I didn't want to bring up what I had researched or what Sierra had told me right away. Sierra was still home, and she was waiting for her father, Nigel, to come and pick her up for the weekend. I didn't want to start a full-fledged argument with Justin and have Sierra worried that it was her fault.

Nigel came into the house to pick up Sierra. He knows me very well, and he could tell that I was bothered by something.

"What's wrong with you, Bree Bree?"

"Nothing," I said with a fake chuckle.

"Uummm hmmm, yea, okay." I was relieved that Nigel let it go; he picked up that this was not a good time to talk.

I quickly shifted the conversation and mentioned how excited Sierra was to spend the weekend with him, as they were going to an amusement park. At that time, Sierra rushed in. She anxiously grabbed her overnight bag, ran over to kiss Kennedy, said goodbye to Justin, and gave me a kiss before she went out the door with her father.

As soon as Sierra and Nigel left, I started to get Kennedy ready for her dinner, bath and bed. I was expecting our conversation to get heated, and I wanted to make sure that Kennedy was tended to before I got too overwhelmed with emotion and stress. Justin could tell that something was wrong with me, but he did his best to avoid asking me what was going on. He kept sighing and talking about what a long day he'd had at work. I could not have cared less about how his day at work was. My mind was set. *We are having this conversation tonight!*

Kennedy fell asleep with no hesitation at all. I actually chuckled to myself, watching her in her crib sleeping so peacefully, like a little angel. It was as if she knew that her cooperation was greatly needed tonight.

I waited until Justin came out of the shower to begin our discussion. I could tell that he knew I wanted to speak with him. He plopped on his side of the bed and sighed.

"What's up, Bree?" he asked in a tone that signaled he was dreading the conversation. "What's on your mind?"

I matched his tone with sarcasm. "As a matter of fact, something *is* on my mind. Soooo... I was online today looking at our cell phone bill, and I noticed a lot of phone calls between you and your kids' mother for long lengths of time. In addition to that, there were other females' phone numbers that you called and also talked to for long lengths of time."

"How do you know the other numbers are females, Bree?" he questioned.

"I'm glad you asked. I called them and listened to their voicemails, which also referenced their names." I paused to let that information sink in before I hit him with another body shot. "There were a couple that answered, and I disconnected after verifying that it was a female."

"Bree, have you ever considered that maybe it was a wrong number?" Then, he chuckled as if I was a juvenile. That infuriated me, so I went for the knockout punch.

"I printed our cell phone bill and took the liberty to highlight the phone numbers and talk times, Justin!" Then, I flung the evidence on the bed where he was sitting. "Surely," I said, "you weren't talking to a stranger or a wrong number for 30 to 45 minutes daily!"

Justin was pissed. In his anger, he did the unthinkable: he started to yell at me the same way that he did his kids' mother, disrespectful and full of rage. When Justin is backed into a corner, he always comes out fighting. I just never thought that *I* would be his opponent. I truly believed that the rage I had observed in the past was specifically reserved for his kids' mother because of who she was and how she conducted herself. I had put myself on a higher pedestal than her, and I'd assumed that Justin had done the same, viewing me with a greater level of respect, value and regard. Apparently, I was wrong.

Justin yelled so loudly that he woke up Kennedy. Sensing his level of rage, I was too scared to bring up the most important topic, the one about which Sierra had told me. My broken spirit allowed me to be overwhelmed by Justin, silencing me and my feelings. In this state, I wasn't able to connect the dots from each of the writings on the wall that I had seen in the past. If I'd had the courage to truly see and acknowledge these writings on the wall, these red flags, these warning signs, I would have recognized that this was all a part of a dysfunctional pattern that needed to be addressed rather than ignored.

six

Hide

A couple days passed after our big argument without Justin and I saying a word to one another. When Sierra returned back home from staying at her father's house all weekend, I was sure that she could clearly feel the tension in our home. Although she'd *felt* the effects of the aftermath in the atmosphere, I was grateful that she had not actually *seen* that side of him. It was bad enough that she had already witnessed him peeping at me.

A week passed with Justin and I only managing to say the bare minimum to one another. I was miserable. Then, Justin came home one evening with flowers and a thoughtful card that read in big bold letters, "I'M SORRY." He assured me that I was the only one whom he loved and that he had proven it by marrying me. He agreed that the additional conversations that he'd had with his kids' mother were not cool, but he also justified that the majority of the conversations had to do with their kids.

"And the other random phone numbers, Justin?" I asked. He wasn't getting off that easily.

"No excuses, B. I got caught up in the moment, questioning myself and whether I still had it. I was trying to find out if other women still found me attractive. I know it was wrong, and I'm sorry, so I'm extending an olive branch. I'm willing to change my phone number to prove to you that I am trustworthy. Let's leave the past in the past, please?"

A broken person with a broken spirit accepts broken actions. Throughout this ordeal, I kept hearing the voices of those who had warned me before we got married saying, *Marriage is hard!* Thus, I felt that I was expected to endure these hardships with my husband, as brutal as they were. I kept telling myself, *Bree, this, too, shall pass. You didn't get married to get a divorce. We can survive this.*

I was determined for Justin and I to move forward from this storm in our new marriage. I still had not mentioned what Sierra had told me. I prayed over the situation and decided that she had probably misinterpreted what she'd seen. After all, she was only 11 years old – a kid. Justin was only looking at me, and I was his wife, so there was no problem.

Therefore, I gave in, accepting Justin's apology, taking him up on his offer to change his number as a sign that he could be trusted, and leaving the past in the past. Little did I know that in years to come, Justin would go on to change his number a few *more* times due to his indiscretions. His old familiar motto, "Leave the past in the past," would also come back to haunt me in the future. The truth was that the reason Justin had always wanted to leave the past in the past was because the past contained everything that he wanted to hide from me.

God has a way of speaking to His children. In the beginning, it could be a whisper, like Him using the lady at the parole office or Sierra, for example, to try to get my attention. Then, when we ignore the whisper, it graduates. I know God knew that I was His hard-headed child who refused to acknowledge His whisper. By the time God was through with me, He would be yelling!

I had continued to apply for new jobs and was soon offered a position at a company to which I'd applied. It was a job working in the same industry that I had been employed in for the past five years. I was excited! Not only did the position offer more money, but it was a closer distance to our apartment than my previous job. However, the best thing about the new job was that it was just down the street from Scharae's job, and it was in the same city where she lived, too! *This will give us the opportunity to have lunch together and meet up after work!* I thought. I was so excited to go back to work after eight months of staying home with Kennedy. I was ready to get up, get dressed, and speak to adults again! I was going to miss my baby dearly, but I needed a change of scenery.

To be completely honest, I too, looked forward to getting out of the house so that I could see if other men were still attracted to me. Of course, I would not go to the extremes that Justin did and actually collect phone numbers and converse with them. However, a friendly compliment or smile from an attractive man would be a nice affirmation that I still 'had it.'

Orientation day for my new job was approaching fast. I made a hair appointment with my stylist, Tiffany. Sitting in her chair was the equivalent of lying down on a therapist's couch! She asked how the girls were doing, and how married life was going.

I replied, "The girls are wonderful, and married life is challenging." Tiffany, who had been Justin's best friend when they were younger, and she still often affectionately referred to him as one of her best friends in their adult years. Hearing that married life was challenging with her best friend got an immediate response out of her. She swiftly spun my chair around so that I was facing her.

"*What* did that fool do?" she asked with concern. We both started to laugh, because she knew him well.

I told her about the mobile phone bill with random numbers and extra calls to his kids' mothers. Tiffany agreed that my anger was justified and said that she would also be pissed if her man had done such a thing.

The dynamic of the relationship that Tiffany and I shared was special: she knew both me and Justin, and she knew us not only as a couple but individually. When confiding in Tiffany, I didn't feel judged or on the fence about what or how much to share with her, because she loved us both; she wasn't going to unfairly take sides. This was unlike the level of information that I could share with my besties, Scharae and Mia, who at times seemed more skeptical of Justin, because their first concern was looking out for me.

My hair was completed, and I have to say, I was cute! Tiffany always successfully slayed my hair. There's nothing like a new hairstyle and new employment to change how someone views themselves.

As I look back on this season of my life, I can clearly see how the enemy has a way of camouflaging and distracting people from the truth. He had been very successful in this season with me. I had no idea that this was happening; I thought because my family and I were present in church most Sundays that we were fine. Little did I realize that I had intentional blinders over my eyes, placed there by the enemy, so that I could not see the truth. I had no idea – no idea at all.

The night before my first day of work, I was feeling very excited to start a new phase of my career, and I was grateful for the opportunity to make my own money again. Justin was happy for me as well, but I could also tell that he was concerned. I believe that he had grown quite comfortable with me always being at home and wearing sweatpants, my hair in a messy bun.

The next morning, I woke up with a zest for the future and anticipating great things to happen. I was upbeat and enthusiastic as I got myself ready for work and also got Kennedy ready to go to daycare. We had been blessed to be introduced to Scharae's family friend, who was a childcare provider. The woman also attended Scharae's church, so my bestie knew her well. Scharae raved about the woman's child care skills and had referred me to her to watch Kennedy during the day as I worked.

When I met the woman, I felt comfortable at once. Her spirit was kind, but old-school. Justin and I agreed that we wanted her to be Kennedy's child care provider when I returned to work. I was going to miss my baby during the day, but I knew getting back to work was necessary; we had outgrown our little apartment, and we were trying to find a bigger place, hopefully a house. After dropping Kennedy off at her daycare, I headed to my new job.

After I was checked in at my new job, I was escorted to a training room, where other new hires were gathered. In walked a familiar-looking face. I recognized her face, but I had never known her name. As I was trying to recall where I remembered her from, she looked at me, and I could tell that she was trying to do the same. We knew each other; we just could not figure out from where. We smiled at each other. It turned out that she had also worked at my old job and had been hired at this new job on the same date as me.

Her name was Charlie, and she had a gentle and kind personality. I loved how silly she could be at times while still being quite intelligent. She and I became very close in the years to come. I affectionately called her "my kindred," because I felt like we had kindred spirits. Charlie became one of my best friends; the chemistry of our sisterhood was evident. Scharae and Mia both really liked her as well.

Once I began working, the extra money that I was able to contribute to the household was great. Justin and I found ourselves going away for the weekends together, going out to eat with our family more often... just enjoying life. Before long, we noticed that we had been spending a bit too frivolously and that we needed to make a plan and a budget to save up so we could move.

The beauty of how Justin and I operated together is that when we set our minds on achieving something together, we always seemed to work together well to attain the goal. It seemed like when we embarked on something new and tried to be focused on a goal, everything would fall into place right before our eyes! Therefore, with the goal being to move into a house, we established a budget, made a plan, and stuck to it.

Still, in the back of my mind, the information that Sierra had shared with me still lingered. To try to 'fix' the situation, I purposely began taking showers with the door wide open so that there would be no need for him to peep in on me. However, while this might have helped to address one problem, others arose.

I discovered that Justin had picked up the bad habit of watching porn. When I asked him about it, he would simply say, "All guys watch porn, Bree! You're making too much out of it."

At first, I wondered if I really was making a mountain out of a molehill. That lasted until our home computer started to get viruses due to Justin searching for X-rated material online. I couldn't even let Sierra use our home computer in fear that something vulgar would pop up. Now, I *knew* that I had not been overreacting to the situation. Justin's appetite for pornography had become a problem that was affecting the entire family.

During this time, I also began to doubt myself, particularly my abilities to satisfy my husband's seemingly insatiable sexual appetite. Even worse, I began to wonder if he was in the moment with me when we were sexually intimate or whether he was thinking of a woman he'd seen on a pornographic DVD or on the internet.

Again, I decided to 'fix' things by increasing the frequency and sensuality of our sexual encounters. However, before long, all of the extra activity began to leave me feeling tired and run down. I wasn't making love to my husband because I had the urge to; I was doing it to make sure that I was fulfilling him so that he wouldn't go out looking for another woman. I was also doing it to prove to him that he did not need to watch porn on a screen when he had a wife who was willing to actually give him the same experiences in real life. I was the real thing, not a fantasy!

One morning, as I talked to Scharae and Mia on our daily conference call, I was complaining to them about how Justin had an annoying interest in porn.

"How long does it take for a man to grow out of this?" I asked.

They both admitted that they had dealt with the same monster at some point in their relationship. I felt relieved to know that I was not in it by myself. *This is just a phase*, I thought. *I just have to be patient until he grows out of it.* We all laughed at how tired a woman can become with a man that has a huge appetite for sex!

Jokingly, Mia said, "Just be glad you haven't gotten *pregnant*!" We all started to laugh out loud. Then, I stopped. I started to frown, because I couldn't remember getting my period that month.

"Hey, did you guys start?" I quickly asked them.

"Yes!" they both confidently answered. I felt sick. The three of us are in sync with our cycles. We always started either a day before or after one another. They both had their cycle at the beginning of the month, and I had not had my cycle since the previous month.

Hearing my silence, Mia started to bust up laughing out loud, while Scharae tried her hardest to mask her giggle from me. I was so mad that I was completely speechless. I just released my call and hung up.

I called the office and advised them that I was going to be late, because I was not feeling well. I dropped Kennedy off at her daycare and headed straight to the nearest pharmacy to get a home pregnancy test. After I purchased it, I went straight home. I was glad that Sierra was at school and that Justin was at work. For this, I needed total privacy.

Before I took the test, I kneeled down and prayed to God as if He was my personal genie. Isn't it funny how we only call on God when we are in a bind? When our backs are against the wall and we have no answers ourselves? When only *He* can fix the situation?

Maybe I didn't pray well enough or long enough; the test was positive. In tears, I called Mia.

"I'm *pregnant*, Sister!" I cried. She could tell that I was clearly distraught.

"What are you going to do? Did you tell Justin yet?" she asked.

"No, you are the only one who knows that I'm pregnant," I said between tears. The reality of the situation set in. "We can't *afford* another baby! We're saving up money to move into a bigger place, and this will set us back *big time*! I just started this new job. To take a leave of absence so early in my employment would be *awful*! I get really sick when I'm pregnant, and the thought of going through months of sickness again is for the *birds*!" I rambled near frantically.

Attempting to soothe me, Mia replied, "God doesn't make mistakes. A baby is a gift from God. You're married, Sister. What option do you have other than keeping the baby and trusting God? You know that you're an extra sensitive person. I don't think you would be able to live with yourself if you aborted it," she calmly reasoned.

"What choice do I have, Mia? To me there are more negatives than positives," I replied. However, there was also the thought in the back of my mind, *What if this is my son?* I'd really wanted a boy. In fact, I was secretly praying for a boy when I was pregnant with Kennedy. However, after Kennedy was born, although I was over-the-top in love with my beautiful baby, that was it. I'd never envisioned myself having another child. I was satisfied with my two girls.

I called my workplace and told them that I would not be able to make it in that day because I was ill. Then, I called Justin at work and asked if he could come home for lunch. He wanted to know why I was still at home. I told him that I would explain it to him when got there. From this, he could tell that it wasn't great news. He wanted to know what he was being accused of now.

"Nothing, but is there something that you would like to share? Then, by all means, please, enlighten me!" I responded. *This is another reason that I don't want to be pregnant,* I said to myself. I believed that Justin had done the majority of his cheating when I was carrying Kennedy. I couldn't prove it. I just had a feeling.

When Justin came home for lunch, I was sitting on the couch.

"What's up?" he asked. "Why was it necessary for me to come home for lunch?" Rather than answer him, I showed him the pregnancy test.

"Woah! It's positive!" he said.

"Yep, it sure is," I said, as I immediately started to cry. He tried to comfort me as best he could. "What are we going to do?" I asked. Justin just looked at me. Breaking the silence, I asked, "Do you want any more kids?"

"Not really, but it appears that we have one on the way," he said.

I began to tell Justin all of my concerns that I had shared with Mia earlier. Then, I asked, "What about an abortion?"

"That would be your decision, Bree."

I resented that Justin had placed the burden of such a decision solely on me. We had both made this baby. I was not his girlfriend or some random female that he'd accidently knocked up. Justin looked at his watch and mumbled that he needed to get back to work. He gave me a kiss on my forehead and left.

For the next two weeks after learning that I was pregnant, Justin became very distant. It seemed almost as if he was being distant on purpose. I felt that he was okay with me getting an abortion, but he didn't want to encourage me to do so because it would make him come off as the 'bad guy.' It was easier for him to say, "It's your body, so it's your decision." He was not the only person at fault; I blamed myself the most for not trusting God.

The most ironic part of this pregnancy was that after I found out that I was pregnant, I was not sick – no nausea or dizziness, and I wasn't even spotting. My only symptoms were that I was hungry all the time and extremely exhausted. The only ones who I told about the pregnancy were Mia, Scharae, Roxy and Charlie. I deliberately didn't tell Michelle, who is Kennedy's godmother. Recently, Michelle had excitedly informed me that she and Jack were expecting their second child together. If she had known what I was planning to do, she would have been so disappointed in my decision. I also thought that if she knew, she would do her best to try and talk me out of it. I did not want to upset her, and I didn't want to feel judged, so I did not share the news with her.

The morning of my scheduled procedure, I was a ball of nerves. Justin took me to the appointment, but not once did either of us bring up the possibility of changing our minds. We both were silent on the way to the appointment.

I can recall two occasions that morning when I believed that the Lord was talking to me. The first was when we got to the clinic; there was a small group of pro-life protesters carrying picket signs that read "A baby is a gift from God." That caught my attention, because I remembered Mia saying that same thing to me the morning I found out that I was pregnant.

The second time when I believed God that was talking to me happened when I was inside of the clinic. I'd just assumed that they took cash so that patients could keep their names confidential, so cash was all I'd brought. However, when we checked in, I was told that a cashier's check was needed for me to have the procedure. Justin and I had to leave to find a store that would provide me with a cashier's check.

As we were leaving the clinic, the protestors noticed that I had gone into and come out of the clinic quickly; they assumed that I had changed my mind. They started to cheer for me and chant, "Thank you, Jesus!" I ducked my head and walked quickly to our car. Justin and I looked at one another but said absolutely nothing to each other. We drove to a 7-11 store, purchased a cashier's check, and made our way back to the clinic. Needless to say, I was booed when I walked back into the clinic.

The procedure was so dehumanizing; I felt like an animal. A group of girls sat in a waiting room, waiting to have a God-awful procedure performed on them. I was one of the girls. When it was my turn, they called me back into the room. The procedure was quick. I woke up feeling very woozy from the anesthesia. I felt empty.

My heart was broken, but I didn't want to disclose my feelings to anyone. I can remember crying by myself for about a week after the procedure. I never shared that emotion with anyone. I asked God for forgiveness over and over again, although I knew that when I asked the first time, I was already forgiven. The other pleas were for me to help forgive myself.

Two weeks after the procedure, I contacted my OB-GYN to schedule a tubal ligation surgery. I was never going to go through that trauma again. I ended up having my tubes tied in order to prevent any future pregnancies. I was determined to not repeat the same mistake twice.

The heartbreaking part of me aborting my child was that two months after I completed the procedure, Justin and I found a beautiful three-bedroom house with two-and-a-half baths, a family room, a formal dining room, an attached garage, and both front and back yards. The only downside to our new home was the distance from my parents' home and from our jobs. If only I had trusted God! If I'd had a stronger relationship with Him, I would have had no reason to fear the unknown. I would have known that all things would work together for my good.

Nonetheless, my family and I were growing excited about moving to our new house. I believed that making the move was a sign that our best years were before us. Again, I was wrong. To my dismay, the new house to which we were moving would be the birthing place of not only my darkness, but others'.

Although Justin and I were excited about our big move, ever since the abortion and my tubal ligation procedure, we seemed to have grown distant from one another. We both thought that this move was just what we needed to get us out of our rut; it would help us to begin a new chapter of our lives together. I was very hopeful for our future. *New home, new memories!* I kept saying to myself. I was filled with optimism.

The morning of our big move, the phone rang at 7 a.m.

When I answered, my girl began to sing, "It's the first of the month, get up, get up!" by rap group Bone Thugs & Harmony. It was Roxy! She put a huge smile on my face, and I was so fired up about our move that I began to sing with her! We both started to laugh.

"Hey girl! You guys ready for the big move today?"

"Yes ma'am! We are. J already started, and me and the girls will leave shortly for the new house. Just making sure everything is gone from here before we leave," I said.

"Well, I can only imagine how busy you are, so I won't hold you up. Congrats again, Friend, and I will see you later tonight. Can't wait to see your new home!" she exclaimed.

"Okay, girl. Thanks. See you later tonight!" I felt blessed to have supportive girlfriends like Roxy in my life.

The move took all day. We were extremely tired, but we were excited. Our house was *so* big, and we both felt proud and accomplished, coming from a small two-bedroom, one-bathroom apartment into this! My parents had to admit that Justin had done a great job of upgrading us, and they were quite impressed with this major milestone for our family. It was so nice to have my family and close friends over the night of the move to celebrate with us.

That night, I could tell that Justin was overwhelmed with emotion; he disappeared from the family room where we were all gathered. I excused myself from my friends and family and went upstairs to search for him. I found him in our master bedroom. He was teary eyed.

I asked him what was wrong.

"Nothing is wrong," he said. "Actually, everything is right." I held him and professed my love for him.

That was the first time after the accusations of cheating, the abortion, and what Sierra told me that Justin and I felt solid again. I convinced myself that we would leave all the bad things at the old place and create beautiful, loving memories here at our new home. It would be a fresh start with no looking back! Little did I realize, once again, that I was so *ignorant*! For me to be such an intelligent woman, I had displayed stupidity at its highest level. In this moment, I'd had no idea of how bad things were going to get in this new home.

Justin and I both took a week of vacation off from work to get settled in to our new home. There were also logistics to discuss: we had to talk through our schedule for the kids, Sierra's school drop-off, and our work routes. Our house was quite a distance from both of our jobs, Sierra's school, and Kennedy's daycare. We sacrificed proximity to these areas for the sake of living in a large house in a nice community rather than living in an apartment.

I didn't want to take Sierra out of her school in the middle of her school year. Since my parents' house was only a couple of blocks away from her school, my father was still able to pick her up after school. Justin worked in the same city as Sierra's school, so after he got off of work, it made sense for him to pick her up from my parents' house. Then, they would both come home together; Sierra would be his carpool buddy on the commute home. Kennedy's daycare was in the same city where I worked. Thus, I would pick her up after my work day ended, and she would be my carpool buddy on the way home. It sounded like a great plan to me.

We gradually began to adjust to our morning schedules. Each morning, Justin got up at the crack of dawn to get ready for work while the girls and I were still asleep. To me, he had the best schedule, because he got up in peace and left in the same manner, only being responsible for himself. My schedule was the complete opposite.

After I got up, not only was I responsible for getting myself ready, but I had to get a busy toddler and a pre-teen ready for school. My routine was *far* from smooth and peaceful. It involved a lot of crying, yelling, arguing and moodiness. I felt as if I was in a constant war zone every morning! I battled to leave the house at our scheduled time, and I battled traffic going to my numerous drop-offs. I had to drop off Sierra at her junior high school, then jump back on the freeway to drop Kennedy off at the daycare, then shoot straight off to work. By the time I got to work, I was already exhausted! Then, I had to muster up the energy to give my job 110% for the next eight hours! We worked this schedule for months. I was grumpy and tired, but every night when I pulled into the two-car garage of our big beautiful house, it was all worth it.

Over time, I started noticing that Sierra had begun to seem very needy. However, I chalked it up to her going through typical pre-teen emotions. Every day, around 3:30 or 4:30 p.m., she would call me and ask me what I was doing. This would totally annoy the hell out of me, because she knew darn well that I was at work until 5:30 p.m. and that Kennedy and I would not get home until after 7 or 7:30 p.m. due to the traffic. She would always end the call by saying something like, "Hurry home!" and "I love you!"

When I would finally get home, Sierra would be super clingy. I would come in and ask her if she had done her chores, and she always said she'd completed them. Every day, Justin made sure that Sierra followed her schedule to the tee. Her schedule, according to Justin, was that when she got home, she would take a shower, do her homework, and then wash the dishes – in that order, always. I thought that it was a great schedule that would teach Sierra to discipline her time and take care of her responsibilities.

Additionally, I began to notice that every day, Sierra would ask to stay longer at my parents' house. She also began to ask if she could spend the night there more often. Of course, my parents were okay with it; she was their grandbaby and always welcomed. My dad would call me while I was at work to ask if Sierra could stay over for the night.

"No," I would flat out say. "Justin and I are trying to teach her discipline and order, and she just doesn't want to do any chores."

I said this because in my parents' home, Sierra was waited on hand and foot. I did not agree with that level of being spoiled, so I would generally not comply with my father's requests. Sometimes, I would give in, but when I did, Justin would usually get upset with me, saying that I was not being tough enough on Sierra. He would request that she come home and stick to her normal schedule.

A few months passed, and Sierra was getting worse with her requests to stay at my parents' house. One day, I told her not to go home with Justin. I told her to wait for me so I could pick her up after work and we could talk on the ride home. I could feel that something was wrong with her; I just wasn't sure of what it was.

When I picked Sierra up from my parents' house that day, we got in the car and started our long journey home.

"What is going on?" I asked her.

She said that she did not want to be picked up by Justin anymore.

"Why?" I asked.

"Mommy, he always does a lot of work in the attic when I am in the shower," she said.

"That's strange," I replied. "Does he say what he's doing?"

She shook her head. "No."

At that moment, I felt a tug in my stomach. However, I managed not to show Sierra my concern.

"Sierra," I began, "I noticed that the shower curtain in your bathroom is missing. I meant to ask you a while ago but it slipped my mind. Did you do something to it?"

"No, Mom. Justin took the curtain away. He said it was filled with mildew and he needs to buy a new one," she replied.

"So how do you take a shower?" I asked.

"I take a shower without having the water very powerful or I take a bath. Justin also told me that I can't close the vent for central air and heat in my bathroom and bedroom. He said it must always remain open so that it doesn't break the system when he is running it."

There were a lot of questions in my mind, like *Why have I not heard a word about him working in the attic?* Typically, he would mention something like that to me; he'd always wanted kudos for doing anything in the house. Also, *Why would he take the shower curtain from Sierra's bathroom?* As I silently contemplated the questions in my head, Sierra tapped my hand.

"Mommy?"

I turned to look at her. "Yes, Babe?"

"The other day when he said he was going to his friend's house and told me to take my shower then do my chores, I thought he left when I jumped in the shower. But when I got out of the shower, I went to your room to put back a shirt that I borrowed. I walked into your master closet, and when I went in, I looked up and I saw his foot hanging out of the ceiling. I thought he was gone! I ran out of your room and went into my room so he wouldn't notice that I saw him. About five minutes later, he opened the garage door and came upstairs like he was gone that whole time. I think he's looking at me, Mommy, the same way I saw him looking at you! Can you please allow me to stay at Grandma's and Grandfather's house until you get off work? And you can pick me up when you are off work? *Please*, Mom?" My daughter was pleading with me.

A blank stare covered my face and I felt a hole in my soul. *This feels so unreal,* I thought.

"Mom, can I?" she persisted.

I snapped out of my daze. "Of course. No worries, Baby, that's fine." I could immediately see the look of relief that came over my baby's face.

I, on the other hand, felt sick. Now, as I sat in traffic inching my way home, what seemed like a thousand questions flooded my thoughts. *How do I address this with Justin? Why is this happening? Maybe Sierra is confused... but why would she make this up*? I know my child, and I know when she is telling a fib. It is not even in her character to make up something this sensitive.

The questions that were jumping around in my head resulted in me quickly getting a migraine. Sierra could obviously see that I was concerned, but her undying love and loyalty to me caused her to comfort me. The roles were clearly reversed. She mothered me when I should have mothered her.

We pulled up to our so-called "dream home," but it felt more like a nightmare on this particular day. After I parked the car, I looked her directly into her eyes, held her pretty little face in my hand, and assured her that I would take care of this. Looking into her eyes, I could see that there was more that she had to say, but out of my selfishness, I didn't press her; I could not handle hearing any more at the moment.

"Do you trust me, Sierra?" I asked.

"Yes, Mom. I do," she replied. I gave her a kiss, and we walked in the house.

When I walked into our master bedroom, Justin nervously fumbled for the remote; he was trying to change the channel from the porn that he had obviously been watching.

"Hi, Babe!" he said cheerfully.

"Hey," I responded.

"What's wrong with you?" he asked.

For a moment, I said nothing. Then, I said, "For your information, the plans have changed. I will now pick up Sierra after work."

"What? Why?" he said, obviously a bit aggravated.

"Why are you so bothered?" I asked, watching him closely.

"Well, Bree, she's *my* carpool," he said, trying to sound cool.

"Well, not anymore," I said. "She will stay at my parents' house, and I will get her."

"So, now she has no schedule, no responsibility, nothing," he said.

"Of course she does. She will complete her homework at my parents' house and complete her chores when we come home. She will shower when she gets home with me." I looked him dead in his eyes to see his reaction. "Either battle the traffic out yourself or get a carpool buddy from work," I said.

Justin was upset.

"What going on in the attic?" I asked.

He looked confused. "What do you mean, Bree?"

"Yeah, apparently you've been doing a lot of work in the attic lately when you come home from work."

"Oh yeah. I thought I heard something up there, so I went up to check it out. I think there's a mouse or something up there," he explained.

"Really? Hmmmm," I responded. "And are the central air conditioning and heat working alright?"

"Yes. Why?" he asked.

"Well, Sierra told me that you advised her not to close the vents, because it could break the system. I told her that was nonsense! Especially when a person showers and someone is working in the attic, the vents should be closed, because one might be able to gain visibility into the bathroom if the vents are open. *Surely* you would agree with me, right Justin?" I was completely sarcastic in my tone, and I had intentionally used general verbiage that allowed me to allude to, but not directly accuse him.

The way that Justin looked at me was telling. At that moment, I felt more certain than before that something was going on, but I did not have a clue about the extent of what had been happening. An awkward silence filled our master bedroom for what seemed forever.

"What did you do with the girls' shower curtain?" I asked, my voice breaking through the silence.

"Ahhh... ummm... I had to throw it away. I can get a new one. It had mildew on it," he answered awkwardly.

"How long ago did you throw it out? It seems like it's been missing for a few months now," I said. Every time I had cleaned the girls' bathroom, I'd meant to ask what had happened to the curtain or to simply replace it, but it had always slipped my mind. After his long silent pause, I didn't wait for an answer. "No worries. I'll make sure that I pick up a new one tomorrow after work," I said. Those were the last words I spoke to him that night.

Clearly, during my line of questioning, Justin should have realized that my questions were rhetorical; I could not have cared less if he answered. I was thinking out loud, but I wanted *him* to hear my conversation that I was having in my head. That night in bed, he rolled over towards me, but I had no desire to be touched by him. I continued the silent treatment with Justin for the next couple of days.

Picking up Sierra from my parents' house worked out well, because it also allowed me to stop in daily and check on my parents myself. Before now, I hadn't felt the need to stop by and check on them myself as often, because I had taken for granted that Justin was doing so each day when he picked up Sierra. I also liked the fact that Justin was developing his own relationship with my parents outside of me by stopping in and seeing them daily. This made me more comfortable about bringing my family around my parents. I could also tell that Sierra was a lot more comfortable and less clingy now that I was picking her up.

One day, my dad told me, "The other day, Justin came over to the house to ask Sierra if she wanted to go home with him, and she said, 'No, I want to wait for Mommy.'"

My dad could see the look of disappointment on Justin's face when he'd heard Sierra's response. He advised Justin that there was no need to ask Sierra to ride home with him anymore and that if anything changed, I would communicate the change of plan to my dad directly.

On the way home that night, I waited for Kennedy to fall asleep in the car before beginning another conversation with Sierra.

"Hey, Babe," I started, "you and I will have to start having check-in conversations, okay? Since the last time you and I talked about your concerns, it looks like you have some more stuff on your mind. Would you like to talk about it?"

She shrugged her shoulders as if to say, "Not really, but I will."

"Has he ever touched you?" I asked.

"No, Mommy. He has never." A huge sigh of relief flooded my spirit.

"Mom, he watches a lot of adult movies. I can hear it loud when I'm trying to do my homework," she said.

"*WHAT*!" I yelled. Then, I quickly tried to regain my composure. I knew that in order for her to feel comfortable telling me more, I had to keep myself together.

"You heard it, Babe?" I asked.

"Yes," she said.

"Hmmm... okay. What else?" I asked calmly.

"One day, we were leaving Grandpa's house, and he asked me if I was having sex, or if I was touching myself. He said it was normal, and all girls go through this time in their lives. He said if I was a virgin, I would have to use my finger to explore myself because I am not active. Mom, I was so uncomfortable, I felt like just jumping out of the car! He said I can talk with him because it might be easier than talking to you. He also asked me if I watched porn, and I said 'No.' He said, 'Let me see your phone.' I saw him typing, and then he showed me the phone. It had porn on it! Mom, I was never on that site! He told me that he wouldn't tell you what was on my phone, when he clearly pulled it up himself!"

I was speechless. I felt nauseated, pissed-off, sad, anxious, confused, and betrayed, all at once. A single tear ran down the left side of my face. I don't know which emotion it was from— anger, sadness, or all of them combined.

I internalized everything that I'd just heard, maintaining a cool, calm composure as I drove.

"I love you," I said to my baby. I promised her that she would not have to worry about it anymore. However, that wasn't the end. She continued.

"Mommy, I think he has a girlfriend or something."

"Why would you say that?" I asked with heightened curiosity.

"Ever since he talked to me about masturbating, I would put my earphones on when I got in the car with him. I would pretend like I was asleep listening to music, just so he would not talk to me anymore. He would be on the phone talking to women. When I heard him on the phone, I would turn off my music and listen to his whole conversation with my eyes closed. He would say some pretty inappropriate things to them, and I think they liked it 'cause they talked daily," she explained. I had absolutely no words!

When we pulled into our garage, I could see that Justin had a load of laundry going in the washer. I got Kennedy out of her car seat, and she immediately bolted to her bike, fussing to ride it. I went to check the laundry. I'd only had my back turned for a half a second when I heard a crash. Kennedy had fallen off of her bike, and her leg was stuck in between the washer and dryer unit. As I rushed to free her leg from the crevice, I noticed that, stuffed in the back was the girls' missing shower curtain.

After freeing Kennedy's leg, I instructed Sierra to take her into the house. Then, I stuck my hand into the opening between the washer and dryer and pulled out the shower curtain. I opened up the crumpled curtain; it was not moldy at all. It was only dusty from being stuffed in-between the washer and dryer. I immediately felt that same jerk in the pit of my stomach. If you don't accept anything else, please accept the fact that God is a Protector and a Revealer; He always ensures that, one way or another, the truth will come out, and He discloses the truth to us for our protection.

I was now convinced that there was a problem. A *real* problem. A problem that I could not dismiss with my optimism or by chalking it up to a misunderstanding. Something was going on, and no, Sierra was *not* confused. I balled up the shower curtain, put it in a bag, and then brought it into the house.

Justin was not home. Lately, he had been staying out longer than usual since he didn't have Sierra as a carpool buddy anymore. His explanation was that he wanted to hang out until the traffic died down some before heading home. Either he wanted me to say, "Okay, then go back to picking up

Sierra to ensure that you are home," or he was now using his free time to talk to his new female friends.

I used the free time that I had without Justin in the house to do a bit of investigating. Again, my assistant was the internet. I was able to once again track phone calls as well as their frequency and their times and dates, and again, I was able to deduce that Justin was being very friendly with other women.

I didn't recognize it at the moment, but in my obsession with Justin, I had chosen to spend these critical hours investigating him rather than taking the time to fully understand and address the trauma that my daughter was experiencing as a result of his inappropriate behavior. Rather than thinking, *I wonder how deeply this has affected Sierra. Will it have lasting consequences? Do I need to get her some professional help to deal with this? What measures am I going to take to protect her?* Other questions filled my head. Questions like, *How can I fix this and keep my family? I've invested everything in this man, and look how he's repaying me. What can I do to bring him to his senses and hold our lives together?* Honestly, trying to fully understand what my daughter was going through and had already experienced was too painful for me. I was comforted by and foolishly rested in Sierra's assurance that Justin had never touched her.

Further, instead of dropping to my knees and asking God for direction or feeding myself with the Word of God in order to arm my family against the enemy, I became embarrassed, jealous, fearful, ashamed, and selfish about my own feelings. I was broken. I had no direction. I didn't know what to do.

Despite not having a fully-developed plan of exactly what to do with the information Sierra had shared with me, now that I knew what was going on, I at least knew how I needed to protect her. My first thought was to reach out to Nigel, Sierra's father, to let him know about the situation. However, I allowed the voice of the enemy to tell me that if I'd shared the information with Nigel, he and everyone else would know that I was a bad mother. The shame would be too great. Plus, I had not yet discussed the situation with my husband, the man to whom I'd made a vow to go through life with, for better or worse. I decided that it was too soon to involve Nigel; I wanted to get a better hold of the situation before I told him about what had happened.

When Justin came home, I was already asleep. He jumped into the shower and came to bed. I rolled over with every intention of having a conversation, but he quickly shut me down.

"We need to talk," I said.

"I'm tired and I have a long day tomorrow," he replied. "Can this wait until after work?"

"No," I said. I wanted to talk now.

"Sorry you feel that way, but it will have to wait. I'm going to bed now." With that, he rolled over and went to sleep.

I didn't get a wink of sleep all night. My mind was exhausted with all that I'd heard and seen. I was secretly relieved that we had not talked that night. Not only did I have a migraine due to all the stress, but I also wanted to talk with my parents first.

When I woke up the next morning, Justin had already left for work. I got up and did my motherly duties, and the girls and I headed off to school and to work. On my way to work, I kept getting this relentless feeling that I should go to my parents' house. I acknowledged that feeling, called in sick, and headed to go see my parents.

My dad was in the living room when I walked into the house. He could tell immediately that something was on my mind.

"What's going on?" he asked.

Before I could stop myself, I began to tell him, in detail, what Sierra had confided in me. He looked at me and said that he already knew; Sierra had disclosed what was happening to him first. I was shocked. Sierra had never mentioned to me that she had told her grandfather.

"Dad, why didn't you come and talk to me?" I asked.

He said that Sierra had begged him not to say anything right away, and he felt that it was necessary for him to keep his promise to her, because she was already scared and confused.

"That's why I would always call you when you were at work to ask if she could stay the night," he explained.

I was a ball of emotions. I was mad at my father for not letting me know, I was mad at myself for not being present enough to be able to tell that Sierra was going through something, and I was pissed that my so-called husband had put our family in this horrible situation.

My dad told me to notify Justin that he was not to come back around their house. The anger in his voice was evident, and the look on his face showed his disappointment with my situation.

"Baby, you know you and my granddaughters are more than welcome to come back home," he said. He kissed me on my forehead and walked out of the living room.

"Thanks, Dad," I silently whispered as he walked away. I felt like the weight of the world was piling up on me.

I still had not yet addressed any of Sierra's accusations with Justin yet. I immediately picked up my phone and sent him a text message.

"WE NEED TO TALK TONIGHT. NO EXCEPTIONS," I typed in capital letters.

Justin simply responded, "Ok." His nonchalant text angered me even more. He did not see any urgency in my text, and had dismissed it with just an "Ok"!

Before I left my parents' house, I went to their bedroom and asked if the girls could spend the night; I did not want my girls to be at home when I addressed these issues with Justin. They agreed that the girls could stay with them that evening. I headed home to get ready for one of the hardest conversations of my life.

As I waited at home for Justin to get off of work, I became very anxious in anticipation of our talk. I fixed myself a cocktail to calm my nerves. This was obviously *the wrong thing to do*, but it is what I had chosen to do to cope; I'd do anything to mask this feeling of desperation and confusion.

It was a few minutes after 6 p.m. when I heard Justin's car pull into the garage. My heart was racing. I felt sick to my stomach. He walked into the room.

"Hey."

I waited a few seconds to respond. I took a deep breath and asked, "Are you ready to talk?"

Justin ignored me and asked, "Where are the girls?"

"They're spending the night at my parents'. I wanted to have a private discussion with you, so I made the decision to have the girls stay the night at my parents' house. I wanted to ensure that we wouldn't get interrupted in the event that our discussion gets heated."

Justin sarcastically chuckled. "I get it. You're in the mood to argue," he said, shaking his head.

"Correction, Justin. I am in the mood for understanding and clarification!" I sternly shot back, my voice rising. He could tell by my expression and the tone of my voice that I was 100% serious.

"Okay, Bree. What would you like to resolve?"

"I have been holding on to some information that was told to me..." I began.

"From who?" he interrupted. I ignored his question. "Here we go with this crap," he continued, annoyed. "So, who am I cheating on you with *now*, Bree?" Justin blurted out.

"Actually, Justin, I'm not even *at* the cheating part yet," I said.

Justin took a deep breath. He had a confused look on his face. "Bree, now I'm lost. So we're not talking about me supposedly cheating? So, what are you talking about? What could it possibly be?" His facial expression had suddenly changed from confusion to a worried frown.

I positioned myself on the bed so that I was able to look directly in his eyes. I slowly but clearly said, "Not only are you peeping at me, you are now peeping at Sierra."

His eyes squinted suddenly, then opened wide. Beads of sweat instantly began to form on top of his nose, and in only seconds, his forehead and neck were becoming drenched with perspiration.

I began to shake; his involuntary reaction spoke volumes. Now that I had finally gotten up the nerve to actually tell him that I knew that this was his truth, the doubt that I had allowed the enemy to convince me of, that Sierra had possibly been confused, was squashed.

"She is *lying*!" He yelled out. "What do you mean peeping?"

"You know what the hell I mean!" I shouted back. "The same thing you were accused of when we were dating!"

"Bree, Baby, she has to be confused."

"Don't 'Baby' me, dude! I'm such a fool! I believed you when you said that they were lying about you. I never asked any questions, I didn't push the envelope when you never went into any detail about what really happened, and now you're looking at *my* baby! You freak! This is all my fault. I am *such* an idiot!"

"I am not doing that! Why are you making this up?" he insisted.

"Really, Justin? Answer me this one question: Why did you talk with her about masturbation?" I watched him closely for a response. Silence filled our master bedroom. I'd never noticed how silence could be so damn loud. "How about you putting porn on her phone and accusing her of watching it, and saying it's alright because you won't tell on her? What about you watching her take showers from the attic?" The accusatory questions were spilling out of me. I was yelling, crying, completely out of control.

"Bree, calm down!" He tried to hold me and comfort me. I pushed his arms from me, totally disgusted with him.

"Don't touch me! She is just a *child*!" I yelled. "It started with you watching me. I am your wife! Why did you watch me? You can have me whenever! Why did you invade my privacy? And then you started invading my baby girl's privacy! What the hell is *wrong* with you?" I felt a migraine coming on.

Justin still did not admit to anything. I reached under my bed and pulled out the shower curtain that had supposedly been moldy and needed to be removed. I didn't say a word; I just held it up.

Justin burst into tears.

"Why, Justin? *Why*?" I pleaded as I watched him cry. I had no sympathy or compassion for him. In my mind, he was just a predator.

"Bree, something is wrong with me," he wailed.

"Hell yeah, something is wrong with you! What... am I not woman enough for you? Or am I too much woman, and your sick ass likes little girls?"

"No, I don't like little girls at all," he defended.

Oddly, I believed him when he said that. With tears flowing down his face, Justin grabbed the neck of his t-shirt to wipe his face.

He took a deep breath and said, "I was abused when I was younger by a family friend," as I listened intently. "I have this thing about watching people when they're unaware that they're not alone. It started years ago, and stopped. After I was violated from my parole, I thought that it went away for good. Then it came back, and I began watching you. I thought it was okay because you're my wife, so I didn't feel so convicted. As far as Sierra, I can say that I am not attracted to her in the least bit, but the opportunity presented itself and I couldn't resist it."

"What the *hell* do you mean 'the opportunity presented itself?'" I yelled. His statement had thrown me into a rage.

Justin bear hugged me and told me to calm down.

"I advise you not to touch me, Justin!" I warned. "So that situation when you went back to jail really happened? After you convinced me to stay with you because they were lying on you? I really believed you!"

At this point, my head felt like two Mack Trucks had collided inside my brain. I was exhausted mentally, physically, and emotionally. My goal had been to resolve the situation by the end of our talk; however, I now had more unanswered questions than I did at the beginning of our conversation.

"I am absolutely tired and have no more energy to continue," I said tiredly. "We need to finish this in the morning."

Justin agreed and made his way back to his side of our bed. He began to take off his tennis shoes with his back towards me. I politely tapped him on his shoulder. He turned around.

"Yes, Babe?"

"Just to be clear, you are not invited to share a bed with me," I said.

"Okay. I'll sleep downstairs on the couch in the family room," he replied.

I shook my head from side to side. "No, you won't!"

"What do you mean, 'No?'" he asked.

"I mean, take your sorry-looking ass to your mama's house or go to one of your jump offs' houses!" I said.

"Bree, really! Jump off?" he responded, as if I was being irrational.

"Yes, jump off. Not only do we need to finish the conversation about you looking at me and my daughter, but I still need to understand the conversations and new relationships that you're still having with these random women!" He glared at me. If looks could kill, I would have been dead.

Justin didn't say a word. He quietly put his shoes back on, grabbed his car keys and said, "For your information, I am going to my mama's." When I heard the garage door close, I started to cry hysterically.

My first thought was to call Scharae and Mia for a 911 conference call. However, my shame and embarrassment would not let me release this information. I told myself that I needed to get a better handle on the situation and gather more information before I could disclose this ugly secret to anyone. *This is my family and my marriage, so I need to fix it... or at least try,* I thought.

This was the moment that I started to allow the enemy to convince me that I was doing the right thing by not telling anyone about the crisis I was experiencing in my life. It was the exact moment when I began allowing the enemy to torture me. I was convinced that I was doing the right thing for my family, but I was actually being tricked by the enemy. If only I had been brave enough to trust God instead of myself! I would have saved me and my girls so much heartache and pain.

What I learned in retrospect was that the enemy's purpose is to confuse us and keep us captive in darkness. God's beauty is that He wants to set people free who are held prisoners to their secrets. In that moment of my life, I did not have the capacity to know and identify with just how much God loved me. I was too self-consumed with my own selfish, pride, trying to hold on to something that He was trying to protect me from all along.

I finally cried myself to sleep. However, I was later awakened by a phone text notification. It was from Justin. It read: "Baby, I love you and my family. I am truly sorry. I can't lose my family. Please don't abandon me. I will do anything to fix this. Can we talk tomorrow, please? Give me the opportunity to make this right, Baby. I'm begging you."

I did not respond to his text; there were no words that could accurately articulate the layers of emotions that I was feeling. Instead, I went to the bathroom, opened my medicine cabinet, and took two huge gulps of Nyquil, just so I could go back to sleep. I needed to rest my mind. I needed assistance.

In retrospect, I understand that I should have grabbed my Bible to get the sense of peace I sought instead of Nyquil. However, I was feeling so much that I just wanted to sleep all of my feelings away. I was praying that I was having a very long nightmare and desperately trying to wake up. However, the reality was that this was my life, and I had to find a way to get through this storm.

After I had finally fallen into a deep sleep, the phone rang. I hesitantly reached over to answer it. In a groggy voice, I was able to muster up a faint hello.

"Hi, Baby Girl," the voice on the end of the line said. It was my dad.

"Hey, Dad," I replied.

I knew that he was calling to check on me. His voice sounded really concerned.

Before he could get a chance to start asking me questions, I asked, "Can I call you back later when I wake up?" I was not ready to have that conversation with my dad, as Justin and I had not resolved anything yet.

"Are you okay?" he asked.

"Yes," I quickly answered.

"Okay. Well then, call me back. We can talk when you're ready."

"Thanks for understanding, Dad. I will. Love you."

"Love you more, Baby Girl."

Two hours later, I heard our garage door opening. I lifted my head off of my pillow; the noise had startled me. I instantly began to feel anxious and nauseated at once. I could hear Justin walking up the stairs and making his way to our master bedroom. He slowly and very quietly opened up the bedroom door. He peeked his head in the door quietly, trying his very best not to startle me.

"Good morning, Baby," he awkwardly mumbled.

I just looked at him, completely ignoring his greeting. His mere presence angered me. I could feel my blood beginning to boil.

Justin cleared his throat and said, "Bree, can I talk with you?" Again, his tone sounded timid and unsure.

I nodded my head yes, but I still did not utter a word to him. Seeing that I was willing to talk, Justin walked into the room and took a seat at the foot of the bed.

"I have to confess something to you. When I was younger, a family friend engaged in some inappropriate actions with me," he said.

"What? Was it a guy?" I asked.

"Hell no," he said defensively. "Not a man. An older woman. She showed me how to do things to her. I was always left alone with her when my parents would go out. At first, I didn't know what to think of it, but it kept happening. I started to feel uncomfortable, so I told my parents, but they didn't believe me." Justin's face was blank, his voice was a monotone, and tears were flowing out of his eyes like a leaky faucet.

"Bree, I honestly believe that my urge to look at people when they think they are alone has to stem from my childhood. Babe, I *never* touched Sierra! I just have this fetish to look at and watch people when they think they're alone. I don't know why. I know that it's wrong, but I can't control the urge," he said, with head hung low.

"So are you admitting that, yes, you were watching me... *and* Sierra? Is this correct?" I asked.

His voice grew weak and faint, and he shamefully answered, "Yes."

I was floored. I actually thought that I was dreaming.

"So when you were on that parole violation, that was true? You were peeping?"

"Yes," he replied, staring directly in my eyes. He continued, "I love my family. I don't want to lose you because of my problem. Please love me enough to help me fix it. Please don't abandon me. I am so sorry that I made Sierra feel that way. I want to apologize to her and let her know that this will never happen again." Now, Justin was crying uncontrollably. I had never seen him this emotional before. He looked both distraught and sincere, all at the same time.

My first and natural instinct was to hold him and calm him down. All I saw at that moment was a little boy in a grown man's body crying for what he had gone through, along with the pain that he'd endured in the past. I hugged him, and we both sobbed.

I remember Justin and I saying something in that moment that Scharae had shared with me in the past: hurt people hurt people. *It really wasn't Justin's fault*, I reasoned. *After all, he didn't touch Sierra. This would be an entirely different story if he had. We can weather this storm as a family. Right?* I thought. At that very moment, I made a decision that I was not going to allow the enemy to break up my family. We needed to fix this. Oops! Correction. *I* needed to fix this.

Entering into my 'fixer' mode, I began to mentally put together a plan. My first step would be to get Sierra and Justin together so that I could talk to her and he could apologize and promise her he would never do such things again. This way, we would be able to move forward in the healing process for our family. Thus, step one was to have a family meeting. *Yes,* I thought. *That's it. That's the answer.*

I still hadn't mentioned the issue of the other women to Justin. I was emotionally drained and did not have the energy to bring up another issue. In my mind, the ugliest issue was out, and in comparison, everything else was irrelevant. I had never witnessed Justin being so fragile, open and honest with me as he had been that morning, discussing the pain of his past. I had never even felt this close to him before. It was strange, yet ironically comforting.

"Don't worry, Babe. I will fix it," I whispered softly in his ear. We hugged each other tightly and then fell asleep in each other's arms. The decision was made. I was going to keep my husband and fight for my family.

Around 3 p.m., we woke up. I took a shower with the door intentionally left wide open. Justin got up shortly after I was out of the shower and he jumped in. I made him some lunch and told him that I would be right back; I needed to have a talk with the girls and my parents before I brought the girls back home.

Before I left to pick up the girls, Justin asked, "Can we pray together?"

I was taken aback by his request. Inside I was secretly smiling as I thought, *See, it's getting better already!* My reply showed my enthusiasm.

"Yes! I think that's a great idea." We joined hands, bowed our heads, and then Justin began to pray:

Dear God, we love You. Thank You for my wife and family. Thank You for Your love for us. God, I have a problem with peeping at others. I can't control it, God. I hate it. I don't want it in my life anymore. Forgive me for what I have done, and please deliver me from this bad habit that hurts my life and others'. I have faith and trust in You and Your power to take it away from me. I pray that You would heal every person that has been affected by my behavior. Heal the hearts of my wife and my daughter. I pray that they would forgive me and accept my apology. Let them know that I never meant to hurt them. I rebuke the devil from my life in Jesus' name. He desires to destroy me by putting this evil behavior in my life, but I thank You, Lord, that my life is in Your hands. Order my steps, Lord. Help me walk where You want me to walk and how You want me to walk, and I will obey. I love You, Lord. In Jesus' name, I pray. Amen.

It was such a beautiful and honest prayer. I could hear the sincerity and the fight in Justin's voice. I walked away from that moment feeling hopeful. I knew that in order to beat this demon, we needed to get back in church and have a meeting with our Pastor. However, I didn't share this idea with Justin just yet. My hope was that he would actually come up with the idea and share it with me. This would be my measurement of his commitment to overcome this dark battle.

On the drive over to my parents' house, I called Scharae and Mia; I needed to confide in my besties and let them in on all that had happened. Unfortunately, I heard the voice of the enemy in my ears discouraging me from sharing the sensitive details about my relationship and family. He did all he could to persuade me to keep things to myself, saying: "Why are you telling them your business? After all, they don't tell you theirs. So, why would you expose yourself? What happens in your house stays in your house!"

Coincidentally, neither of my besties picked up the phone. Although on one hand, this made me feel alone, on the other hand, I felt relieved. Them not picking up the phone meant that I didn't have to share this ugly secret. I could continue in the hide.

When I pulled up to my parents' house, my dad was outside with the girls. Sierra and Kennedy both came running to my car; they were both happy to see their mommy. My dad had a concerned, inquisitive look on his face. I excused the girls and asked them to go check on my mother so that my dad and I could have a moment to talk.

Sierra took Kennedy by the hand. As she was about to lead her away into the house, she looked back at me as if trying to read my body language. I knew that she was anxious, so I nodded with a smile to relieve her anxiety.

Sierra smiled back as if to say, "Thank you."

I gave her a hug and gently said, "Everything is going to be fine, just as I promised."

Sierra looked at me and gently said, "Okay, Mom."

My dad, on the other hand, was not relieved. He wanted answers to the many questions that he'd been holding on to. We had a talk, and the tears flowed.

I told my father that Justin had admitted to having some issues, and that yes, the things that Sierra had told him were actually true.

"So, you mean he's a predator?" my dad asked.

"No, Daddy. That's not what I am saying," I answered defensively.

"Then what, Bree?"

I went on to run down the defense to my dad that Justin was a victim himself. An older woman who babysat him when he was a child had abused him.

My dad wasn't buying the explanation that I was giving.

"Dad, are you listening to gain an understanding, or are you listening to make a rebuttal?" I asked.

He grew stern. "Listen. That is your *baby girl*, my *grand*baby, so forgive me if I am not as sympathetic as you would like me to be," he said.

"Dad, you have every right to feel this way. What I am simply trying to do is wrap my head around it all and come up with a solution. The hardest part is out. He has admitted it. So now, as a family in our healing process, we have to start doing what we need to do so that this doesn't happen again. My main priority is Sierra. Once we can get her back to a comfortable state again, then we can put this all behind us. This would be totally different if he had actually touched her. WE are going to seek some help. I didn't get married to get a divorce, and I do not want to just leave him at a time like this. This is my family and my decision. I just need you to respect and support us through it," I said. I had stated my piece.

"I don't want Justin going back to picking Sierra up after school if you are not present with him. She cannot be alone with him. This is meeting you halfway, Bree. Let me advise you that if my grandbaby tells me that he's peeped at her again, there will be a different outcome. Do you understand me Bree?" He asked firmly.

"Yes, Dad. I do." I hugged him and asked that he please not mention any of this to my mother. "I will let you know how things are going, Dad. Whether good or bad," I promised. This didn't reassure my father at all; he had a blank stare on his face. He wasn't sure of what emotion to display or what disguise to display for my sake.

I went into the house and into my old room to collect my daughters' belongings. Sierra walked in.

"Hey, Mom," she said.

"Hey, Baby," I replied.

"Did he lie or did he tell the truth? Is everything okay?"

I went on to tell Sierra that everything was okay and that yes, he had admitted the truth. She looked shocked.

"Mom, that's weird. Why did he do that to me?" she asked.

"He's sick, Baby. I know, it is weird. He, too, was a victim, and he didn't deal with it when it happened to him at a young age."

She frowned. "You mean someone was looking at him too when he was a kid?" she asked.

"No, Baby. Someone actually touched him," I explained.

"Well, if he didn't like it so much, then why is he doing it to me?"

"Because hurt people, hurt people," I responded.

"So that lady in the office who told you to watch him, you mean she was actually telling the truth? Mom, why didn't you believe her?" Sierra questioned.

"I don't know baby. Maybe out of desperation for love. I never believed that something so ugly could be so true," I admitted.

"So, what's going to happen now?" she asked, looking at me expectantly.

"You, me and Justin are going to have a meeting and get us some help. We are a family, and although ugly things happen, you don't just throw your family away. You fix it. Who is our help, Sierra? Huh, who is our help? Who do you go to when you need help?" I asked.

"You, Mom," she responded, a clear indication that we had missed the mark by slacking off from going to church.

"God, our Savior, is the answer honey. He can fix anything. We will fix this, and you will not have to go through this anymore. Do you trust me?"

"Yes, Mommy. I trust you," she said.

After that, I motioned for her to come and gather her things and get her sister so we could go home.

Sierra took a deep breath and sighed, "Alright."

After kissing my parents goodnight, my two little beauties and I headed home.

seven

Façade

The ride home was really quiet. Kennedy had fallen asleep, and Sierra kept her earphones on for the majority of the trip. I could feel her anxiety rise as we got closer to home. I tapped her leg and assured her that everything was going to be alright.

"Mom, are you still going to pick me up yourself after school?" she asked in a meek and concerned voice. She held her breath awaiting my response.

"Yes, Baby. Nothing has changed. We now know that he has an issue, so we are going to do everything possible to make sure that this is fixed. Sound good?" I tried to sound convincing and optimistic.

"Sounds good," she echoed timidly.

When we pulled up, the house was in complete order. Justin had made a beautiful dinner, the fireplace was on, and the atmosphere of home sweet home was picture perfect. *If only our lives were really this beautiful,* I thought. *If only we didn't have to have this ugly conversation about this dark issue.*

"Hello, ladies," Justin said in a humble tone.

"Hi, Daddy," Kennedy said, all smiles.

"Hi, Baby Girl," he said. "Daddy missed you!" He gave Kennedy a great big hug and kiss while Sierra and I walked past their love fest.

"Mom, I'm not hungry. I'm going to go upstairs to my room," Sierra said.

"Sierra, before you do, I would like to speak to you and your mother first," said Justin.

Sierra looked at me as if she was waiting for me to grant her permission to dismiss his request. I grabbed her by the waist and said, "I think a talk is necessary."

"Momma!" She exhaled deeply, trying to disguise her frustration. I assured Sierra that I was going to be right there and would not leave her. She was aware that I was on her side regarding the violation that had happened against her.

I turned on the Disney Channel to keep Kennedy entertained during our conversation. That was perfect. As soon as she heard the familiar theme song to one of her favorite shows, she started rocking back and forth, and her eyes were fixed to the television in the family room. Justin, Sierra and I went to sit in our formal living room from which we could still see Kennedy, but she could not hear us.

Justin began the discussion around the sensitive topic. He looked solemnly over at Sierra.

"I'm sorry," he said.

I looked at Sierra and could tell that she was unmoved; she was not fazed by his apology at all. An awkward silence fell across the room.

I tried to help Justin narrow things down from just a blanket apology.

"For what?" I asked him with a huge attitude.

"I'm sorry for making you feel uncomfortable with topics that were inappropriate."

"What else?" I asked, feeling even more irritated that I was having to draw things out of him.

He muttered, "For invading your privacy."

Sierra started to cry. She looked over at me. "See, Mommy? I told you."

"I know, Baby," I said, trying to soothe her.

"He saw me naked! That is so *weird*!" she exclaimed to me. Then, turning to Justin, she cried, "I call you 'Dad!' Why would you *do* that to me? I *hated* being alone with you! I never knew what you were going to do to me *next*!" Brokenhearted, she continued to sob.

I hugged Sierra, and again, a rage came over me.

"I hate you!" I yelled at Justin as hot tears ran down my face.

At this point, Kennedy had left her Disney Channel show and had run into the formal living room straight into Sierra's arms to comfort her sister. Now, all four of us, "the family," were in the living room crying together.

Justin moved closer to Sierra but didn't touch her. He spoke softly to her.

"I was abused when I was younger, and I actually know how you feel. I am so sorry that I have mishandled your trust and invaded you and your mother's privacy. I am going to get help. I promise I will never do that to you again. Our family means the world to me. I can show you better than I can tell you. I am begging for another opportunity to make things right for our family." That was one of his famous lines that he would often say to us: “I can show you better than I can tell you.”

Sierra weakly said, “I would still like my mom to pick me up because I do not want to be left alone with you.”

“No problem, Babe,” I eagerly replied.

Then, she turned back to Justin. “How are you going to get help?”

“First, I'm going to go talk to our Pastor. As a matter of fact, we all need to start attending church on a regular basis,” he said. We all nodded in agreement.

“Do you accept my apology, Sierra?” Justin humbly asked.

“Only if you promise to never violate my nor my mother's privacy,” she said.

“I promise, Baby Girl.” Justin extended his arm outward towards her and asked her for a hug. Sierra wiped her eyes and obliged by giving him a hug.

“Justin,” I said, “promise me that you are serious about getting help.”

“Babe, you all mean the world to me. I will do anything to make things right and restore order for our family. Please, just give me the opportunity to show you how serious I am,” he replied.

I believed that Justin was both sincere and serious about his restoration, and I also believed that our family meant the world to him. Sierra believed it too.

She said, “I forgive you.”

Justin cried. We all wept. We left our family meeting rejuvenated, filled with hope and resolution. Sierra and Kennedy headed upstairs to call it a night.

Once Justin and I were alone by ourselves downstairs, I looked him directly in his eyes. “You have forgiveness and transparency,” I said to him. “Do *not* mess this up!”

"You're right, Babe," he said, enthusiastically nodding his head in agreement. "Trust me. I will not mess this up."

Before Sierra went to bed, I went into her room to talk to her alone. I wanted her to know that I was on her team and to reassure her that she was the most important factor.

"Babe, you and I need to have a constant check-in. Do you know what I mean about check-ins? No? Not really?" Reading her expression, I could tell that she needed more explanation. "I mean, if you get that feeling again that Justin is doing that same thing, I need you to let me know immediately. If you feel weird, or concerned, or you just want to talk, I'm here for you. Okay?"

"Okay Mom. I will," she said.

"Sierra, we are going to try to make it as a family. What happens in our house stays in our house. Okay?" She nodded.

I wish that I could take back those words. With that very sentence, I had only prolonged my hiding season! I allowed the enemy to run rampant in my life and in my household. I had no clue of what the magnitude of that sentence really was. Little did I realize that it was an open invitation to the enemy to torture and tear apart my family.

Justin and I began to go on family outings and attend church regularly. At this point, I still had not addressed the cheating allegations. We'd experienced enough drama, and I had desired to have a bit of normalcy back in our lives.

Sierra and I had our secret check-ins about every other month. I never mentioned Justin's issues or our family meeting to anyone. There were numerous instances when I would catch myself from almost disclosing the details of Justin's issues to my besties on my daily conference calls with Mia and Scharae. Each time I did, I'd always felt guilty, because we usually talk out all of our problems with one another to seek each other's wise counsel. I felt that if I'd shared what was happening with Justin, they would judge our situation. However, they didn't agree to marry him; I did. This was my burden to bear, and I felt that I must do so alone, silently.

I have to admit that for about six months after Justin confessed his issue, it appeared that our family was getting back on track. Granted, I never left Sierra alone with him, and she seemed less anxious and more comfortable interacting with us than before.

There was one thing, however, that constantly bugged me: I no longer viewed our dream home as beautiful. It now felt tainted and cursed. Everything annoyed me about the house. Now, I saw it as being too expensive, the commute was too long, and it was too big for me to clean every weekend by myself. I was miserable in it, and now, I was requesting to move. After months of complaining and constant disagreements with our landlord for raising our rent, we decided to move.

Trying not to have to pay rent for a new month, we quickly found a two-bedroom apartment in the same neighborhood for a very reasonable price. I was actually relieved to downgrade back to an apartment. There was less maintenance, it was cheaper, and there was NO ATTIC! It offered a controlled environment to help tame Justin's impulsive issue.

During this time in my life, everything was focused around the unspoken issue. It was a season in which I can remember always being anxious and uneasy. Publicly, Justin and I were always seen as the cute young couple. In our church life I was a proud, happily-married woman. In my work life and in our circle of married couple friends, we were the passionate "ride or die" item. Unfortunately, it was all just a façade.

In our apartment, I honestly felt that the peeping had stopped. I wasn't sure if it was because the confined layout of the smaller space meant that Justin did not have the opportunity to peep on us or whether it was because he had finally been able to resist his urges to do so. However, while I felt like Justin's peeping had stopped, what did not stop were Justin's cheating ways. In fact, they progressed heavily.

I am a firm believer that the Holy Spirit can speak to a woman's intuition and reveal to her that her spouse is becoming disconnected from her. In this season of our relationship, the Holy Spirit gave me a sense that something was going on. As it turned out, Justin became acquainted with an old fling. He was very distant and arrogant towards me. The man I had loved, forgiven, and fought so hard to keep together with his family had once again drifted away after another woman. I was already insecure and broken, but the enemy did his best to totally destroy me and take me out with this situation.

I can recall the day that I discovered whom Justin was having an affair with – this time. It started after Tiffany, my hair stylist, and I kind of fell out.

Justin had begun to make me feel uncomfortable about his friendship with Tiffany by constantly professing how strong his friendship with her was. That my husband always spoke about being so strongly connected to another woman did not go over well with me, not to mention the fact that Tiffany is an attractive woman. I was already very insecure about myself and our marriage, so the smallest comments that Justin made about Tiffany would set me off. Knowing how his words affected me, Justin started to purposely use them to play on my insecurities. Over time, his behavior caused a disconnect between Tiffany and me.

What I did not know was that Tiffany had also been feeling uncomfortable with things that Justin said; he would confide in her about the extra women that he'd had affairs with during our relationship. This made it difficult for Tiffany, because she cared about me. Now she was aware that Justin was cheating on me with no regard, and she didn't like it. Tiffany was caught between a rock and a hard place. She didn't want to be caught up in our drama. As a result, my appointments became less and less frequent.

In retrospect, I can now see why Tiff felt uncomfortable: she knew of some of the women whom Justin was entertaining. Tiff was not a hypocrite; she was disappointed with Justin's actions and his blatant disrespect towards me. Consequently, her relationship with Justin also changed. What I am most grateful for is that there was no love lost between Tiff and I after we parted ways. We had to separate for a season, but she and I would meet up again in the near future. God is a restorer!

Now that I was in-between hair stylists, I reached out to my girlfriend, Roxy, for a referral. I was very particular about who did my hair, because Tiffany was the absolute best. Roxy gave me her girlfriend's contact number. Her name was Angel (yes, this was her real name), and she was exactly that for me – an *angel*! From the moment I met Angel, I felt as if I had known her for a while. Justin also knew Angel from his childhood, but they were not best friends. That was a comforting relief to me; he'd often used his best-friend status with my former stylist, Tiffany, in order to create discord and tension between us. I wouldn't have to worry about this with Angel.

Months passed, and I faithfully attended my standing appointments with Angel every two weeks. I was happy with the service because she had growing hands, much like Tiffany's; she had a gift for being able to care for her clients' natural hair so that it would grow long and healthy. Angel's chair had also started to feel like Tiffany's therapy chair.

During this time, things in our household were very strange. Although Justin had stopped peeping, his cheating ways had increased. On one hand, I was relieved that Sierra was out of harm's way, but on the other hand, my marriage was again endangered. Finding the right balance seemed impossible. Not confiding in anyone about what was happening in our home was also making me miserable, isolated and alone. I found myself internalizing everything!

Trying to talk to Justin was like talking to a brick wall. His whole demeanor changed from being humble and focused on making his family work to being cold, disinterested and nonchalant. He started to hang out with his friends on the weekends rather than his family, and he consistently came home late from work. He also started to go out of town frequently with his "boys"; it seemed like every other month, he and his "boys" planned an out-of-town trip. At first, it didn't bother me; I thought that these little breaks would be good for us, giving us a little space – a little personal time apart from one another. However, the more frequently he left with the "boys," the more suspicious I became.

By snooping around, I found out that Justin was having an affair with a girl from his past. Social media provided me with her name, phone number, the city where she lived, and a photo. I was able to match the contact number she'd listed on social media page with our mobile phone bill.

One weekend, when Justin said that he was away on one of his so-called "boys' weekends," I decided to call him. The plan was to keep him on the phone and listen to what was going on in the background. Then, I called the girl, from a blocked number, of course, to compare what I heard in her background. I purposely called her with back-to-back phone calls to annoy and intentionally frustrate her. Then, I would randomly call Justin and ask him regular questions. After a few calls, I was able to conclude that he and she were together. There was no boys' trip. He was with his jump off – his girlfriend.

After I called his phone for what seemed the thousandth time, I'd succeeded in finally pissing him off just enough.

"What the hell are you doing this morning, Bree?" he angrily answered.

"What are you speaking of?" I responded nonchalantly.

"Why the hell are you playing on the damn phone this morning?" he asked, clearly perturbed.

GOT HIM! I silently said to myself. I had been playing on his jump off's phone, not his. The only way that he could be so annoyed was that he had been there with her having to endure my constant calls and hang-ups!

I commenced to cuss him out; every insulting, degrading word in my vocabulary came out of my mouth. Then, I calmed myself down and asked, "Now that I know you're with your *side chick*, when are you coming home so we can talk?"

He chuckled sarcastically. "For what? Now that you know who I'm with, there's no need to cut our trip short," he said.

My mouth was wide open. I was speechless. I was baffled and confused. He showed no remorse or concern that I was aware of what he was doing or that I knew whom he was with. Truth be told, he actually sounded relieved.

"Now, I'm going to get back to my vacation, and you and I, we'll talk when I get home," he said.

"What home?" I calmly asked.

"Bree, like I said. When I return, we can talk." He hung up the phone.

I was shocked. *Did he really just say that? Did he really just pick her over me? Did he forget how I had his back when I discovered his issue?* I was utterly speechless. I immediately called Scharae, sobbing uncontrollably.

"What's wrong, Bree?"

"Justin is having an affair, and he is out of town with her now!" I cried frantically.

"Does he know that you're aware of him cheating?" she asked.

"Yes! I just confronted him, and he didn't deny it. I even asked him to come home now so we could talk and he said 'No!'" I explained between sobs.

"Oh, hell! Hold on. I'm about to conference Mia in."

"Hey girl," answered Mia as I continued crying in the background.

Scharae led the conversation. "Hey Sister. This fool Justin is cheating again, and now he's on vacation with some chick!"

"How do you know this?" questioned Mia.

"He confirmed everything just now and he refuses to come home until his scheduled vacation is over," explained Scharae.

"N***** and flies," mumbled Mia. "Bree Bree?" she called out to me. I had been silent on the call so far, except for my sobs.

"Yes?" I responded, trying to clear my throat and sound like I wasn't falling apart.

"What are you going to do?" she asked me.

"I can tell you what *he's* not going to do," I said definitively.

"What?" Mia asked.

"He does *not* get to come home to his family after he's been with another woman all weekend! Girls, let me call you back. I have to pack the girls and me up. My parents went on a two-month vacation to Jamaica. I'm going to move to their house until they return. It will buy me some time to think of my next move and allow me to get away from him."

The girls agreed that it was a good temporary fix, so I got busy packing.

As soon as Sierra saw me, she could easily tell that I was emotional and stressed. She did her best to give me some space by attending to Kennedy herself. I was grateful, because I was a wreck. I was so filled with hurt that I was sick to my stomach. I couldn't eat, sleep or think. *How could he do this to me despite all I knew and all that he did?* I asked myself. *Why was I not enough? Why the betrayal? Did he ever consider our vows?* A million unanswered questions flooded my mind.

What bothered me the most was thinking about all of the years that I had already invested into the relationship. The thought that I might have wasted the past several years of my life bothered me to no end. Despite these thoughts and questions that plagued me, I somehow gathered up enough energy to pack all of our belongings and move to my parents' house.

Even though it appeared that Justin's peeping had been under control since we'd moved from our so-called dream home to our new apartment, I was able to detect that Sierra was elated about the move because it didn't include him. She never actually articulated this, but a mother knows her child.

Both the day of the move and the day that followed were a blur. I was an emotional wreck. On Justin's scheduled return day, he called me. I allowed the phone to go straight to voicemail. *All of a sudden, after you spent your whole weekend with this broad doing God-knows-what, now your ass wants to communicate?* I thought. I yelled a resounding *HELL NO!* from the depths of my soul towards the phone.

He kept calling all day. I neither picked up the phone, nor did I acknowledge any of his million text messages. Not one. After a few days of being completely ignored, Justin came to my parents' house very early in the morning. He pounded on the door and demanded to speak with me.

I answered the door and I told him to leave. He refused.

Justin begged me to hear him out. I told him "No." He had been with his side chick all weekend, so he needed to go back to her. We had the conversation at the door with a locked screen door between us. I never invited him into my parents' home.

"This is crazy, Bree. Come home tonight, just you, so we can talk this through. If you agree to that, I'll leave now," he pleaded. I agreed so he would leave; I didn't want his noise to wake the girls or the neighbors up.

Later that evening, when I knew that he was off from work, I sent him a text letting him know that I was on my way to talk. Sierra was about 14 years old now, so she could babysit Kennedy, who was about four years old at the time. I told Sierra that I would be back, and I headed to our apartment.

Justin tried his best to be charming and apologetic. He kept referring to his side-chick as a "broad" and trying to convince me of how little she meant to him. I just listened as he explained to me how much his family meant to him and how stupid and childishly he was acting. He begged me for forgiveness once again.

I can vividly remember being completely broken during this time in my life. Mia and Scharae were definitely sent by God to pour some sense into me. We checked in multiple times a day with one another.

After this affair, there would be more, but for some reason, this affair broke me down to my core. I had the spirit of death. I wanted my life to be over. I could not forgive Justin or move forward anymore. My life was miserable. People thought that we were a young couple with a nice little family, simply going through life's typical challenges, but it was all a façade. A lie. My husband was selfish; He was destroying our family, and it was heartbreaking.

The only saving grace was my two babies; I had to stay alive for them. If I were to check out of life, what would happen to them? Who could love them like I could? Sure, I had some pretty amazing friends – Mia, Scharae, Charlie, Roxy and Michelle – who would step in as their godparents and take care of them, but they were not Sierra and Kennedy's mom. I was. No one could love them or care for them like me.

Social media became my enemy. The woman who had willingly had an affair with my husband, knowing that he was a married man, began to drop subliminal messages on social media: she would post pictures of his body but not his face. She would also make inside jokes with her friends on social media using captions that only certain people familiar with the situation would understand. She would tag her photos with hashtags like #cheapertokeepher and #heisMYman and make comments like "I want to go back on vacation" and "If you only knew." Her friends would LOL, tell her that she was so crazy, and make their own jokes in response to them, all at my expense. Although she never used my name or referred to me directly, she knew that I was aware of her relationship with my husband and that my friends and I had seen her posts. She taunted me and mocked my marriage mercilessly, and this drove me into even deeper despair.

The saying that "the devil comes to kill, steal and destroy" was so real at this point of my life. Death was anxiously knocking at my door, because I did not know my worth. I allowed myself to be consumed with misery. I did not have the capacity to understand that this was a trick of the devil. I was in darkness, and all I could see was dark. I could not see any light anywhere. I had no hope. What made things even harder was feeling that I had to conceal what was happening in my home and my relationship from everyone. I felt trapped and alone.

Eventually, all of the stress that I was experiencing caused my once-youthful look to give way to constantly looking tired, worn down and weary. I was deteriorating. I lost a large amount of weight, my long hair fell out, and my skin became plastered with acne. However, while I was showing physical signs associated with the stress of a dying relationship, Justin was just the opposite. He looked just fine. In fact, he looked like he was doing better than ever.

The mind truly is the enemy's playground. I began to speak aloud all of the negative thoughts I was having and conversations that I was hearing in my head, all prompted by the enemy. *No wonder he cheats. It's because I'm not worthy. I should be grateful that he still wants to be associated with me as his wife,* said the negative, self-pitying voice in my mind.

Hearing my doomed confession only gave the devil more ammunition to destroy my spirit. How could I possibly hear God's voice when I'd welcomed and consumed the devil's lies as truth? I went deeper and deeper into the darkness with a negative mind and a broken spirit.

After several weeks of living in the unbearable darkness, I agreed to move back in with my husband. Sierra was *pissed.* However, I explained to her that this was my marriage so it was my decision; when she grew up and had her own marriage, she could make her own decisions.

"Where is my mom, the one who taught me to stand up for what's right? Mommy, you are not yourself. You deserve so much more!" Sierra pleaded. Her plea fell on deaf ears; my ears were already being monopolized by the enemy. *She's just a child. She doesn't know any better*, I thought. The trickery of darkness is that it keeps you in the dark so that you do not realize that you are in the dark. I was so deep in the dark that there was no reasoning with me. Not even my daughter, whom I love most in the world, could bring me back.

Justin became cocky. Hell, why wouldn't he? My return to him affirmed that he could basically have his cake and eat it, too. All he had to do was offer up a disingenuous apology for whatever he had done to get me back. It always worked.

I thank God for Scharae and Mia. I have always been grateful for their support of me, for their love of my kids, and for our strong sisterhood. Even in this ugly place of darkness, the Lord still showed me His grace through my sisters. They could have easily called me "stupid" and chosen to love me from a distance as I made bad decision after bad decision. However, thankfully, they did the exact opposite.

Our conference calls went from daily to just about hourly, as they both felt responsible for ensuring that I was safe. This was especially a concern because of all of the subliminal messages that Justin's side-chick continued to post on social media; they had me contemplating suicide. I was in so much pain that the only solution I could see to ending it was death. I was now skin and bones, had short, damaged hair, and acne. It was the complete opposite of what I'd looked like a year ago. Of course, only Scharae and I knew what I'd looked like the year before; Mia lived out of state, so she hadn't seen my ghastly appearance. Besides my daughters and my friends, I felt that I had nothing else. They were the only good things in my life.

One day, when I was in my lowest state, I said to Scharae and Mia that if anything were to happen to me, I wanted both Scharae and Mia to look after my girls. I wanted to be assured that if something were to ever happen to me, they knew my instructions for who I wanted to watch over my babies.

"Sure," said Scharae, as if that was a no-brainer. However, Mia heard something different in my tone.

I abruptly got off the phone with them. I went to my medicine cabinet, pulled out all of the pills that I could find, and put them by the side of my bed. I went into the living room, kissed both of my babies, and told Sierra that I was going to take a nap, so keep the noise down.

As I was walking back into my room, the phone was already ringing. The caller ID displayed Mia's name.

I answered. "Hello?"

"B?" she said intensely.

"Yes." For some reason, tears were rolling down my face.

"The Holy Spirit told me to call you back. You are broken, and I can hear the sound of death all over you. Do you know how selfish you are if you are even *considering* ending your life?"

"How did you know?" I asked through muffled tears.

"Bree, God loves you so much! You have no idea how much because you don't love yourself. Justin is not worth you spending eternity in Hell because you feel weak. Your babies need you... and I will kill you *myself* if I get that call! Sister, let's pray." Mia began to pour into me and cover me in prayer. "I bind the enemy from your mind and from your soul." I started to cry out loud, overwhelmed at God's love for me, and in awe that He would supernaturally intervene in my life at such a critical time. Thank God for new mercies daily!

To this day, I have never confessed to Mia that I was actually in the midst of trying to take my life that very moment. A broken heart full of sorrow and hopelessness had been trying to lead me down a path to destruction.

At that moment, I could have also opened my mouth to confess to Mia about the Peeping Tom, but you see, I only had enough strength to disclose what was already out. Everyone already knew that Justin was cheating on me. How stupid would I look if I told the *whole truth*? I was trapped by the devil into believing the lie that I had no other choice but to hide.

By now, Justin and I had been married for five years. *I've invested five years into this*, I thought. *I'm ugly, skinny and insecure. Who else would want me?* Still, I stayed, and more misery set in. From the outside looking in we were just a married couple going through a difficult time. My close girlfriends were very supportive of me trying to love Justin through this rocky portion of our marriage. I still did not utter a word to anyone about the big issue. Instead, I continued to keep our secret. I continued to hide.

Before long, I had a bright idea: we should move out of our quaint apartment into a new place and start over again. Moving would give us the fresh start we needed! As far as I knew, no peeping was happening anymore; only the cheating continued. We found a cute little house for lease on the same street that Justin's parents had lived on for more than 30 years. It was Justin's childhood neighborhood, although I had also been raised in the same city. I thought it was a blessing. What were the odds that we would be able to lease a house on the same street where his parents lived? This would turn out to be anything but a blessing, because I would soon discover this was also the neighborhood in which some of Justin's women lived.

Before we moved, I had a hair appointment with Angel. I told her about the new place into which we would soon be moving. She was aware of Justin's cheating; not only did I often confide in her during my hair appointments, but she'd also heard rumors going around in the city.

A spiritual woman, Angel gave me instructions before I moved. First, she said that I should not move with any dirty clothes, because she believed that spirits traveled in every piece of clothing. She also recommended that all bedding be cleaned prior to moving in. In addition, she said that I should open every window in the new house and go through each one of the rooms reading scriptures, praying and anointing them with virgin olive oil that had been prayed over. Angel said that doing such things was necessary to cleanse my new residence and to ensure that I wasn't bringing any bad energy into our new home.

After Angel had given me all of the instructions, I looked at her, confused. It seemed as if she knew something that she had never disclosed to me. Again, this was another opportunity to open up and free myself from the secret, but I could not find the right words to do so. I fought the urge to share the embarrassing details of my life, gave Angel a big hug, and vowed to do as instructed. Before moving into the house, I did everything she told me to do.

This would be the last house that Justin and I would share as a married couple. The next four years were hell. The enemy, who is calculating, smart and tricky, had his way with me, Justin *and* my kids. It was the darkest of all times. I was defenseless and clueless.

One day, prior to moving into the new house, Justin and I stood outside talking to our new landlord. We were due to move into the house in two days, so the landlord was giving us the 411 on our neighbors. He pointed to the house of one of our neighbors and advised us that she was pretty nosey, so watch out! We all laughed and thanked him for the heads-up. At that moment, this same nosey neighbor walked over to the three of us to introduce herself. We greeted her and told her that it was nice to make her acquaintance.

After the niceties were exchanged, she asked me about what I did for a living? I responded very briefly, telling her where I worked. She then turned to Justin and asked the same question. This offended Justin; he felt like it was none of her business. "I'm unemployed," he responded. I looked up at him feeling so annoyed. I was like, *Why be rude? Just answer the question, geez*!

Although I had been living in the darkness, things had been going well for Justin; he had been blessed with a great job, which he managed to hold for five years with the same company. Despite his shortcomings, I have to admit that he was a great worker and prided himself on taking care of his family. However, this would soon change: two days after telling our new nosey neighbor that he was unemployed, he was fired from his job.

Apparently, Justin had done the majority of his talking to other women while he was at work. He had been warned by the management at his job that doing so was hazardous, because he was handling dangerous material. However, what I took away from the incident was that your tongue has power, so be careful what you say. The enemy can hear your words and will use them against you.

The saying, "An idle mind is the devil's workshop," is one that never made much sense to me – that is, until I began to experience it in my own home. For two years, Justin was out of steady work, so for two solid years, I was the primary breadwinner, working overtime, revamping the budget, and still trying to parent our kids. I was stressed. Of course, this caused additional strain and tension on an already fragile marriage.

To make matters worse, while I was out busting my ass trying to make ends meet, Justin dubbed our new home the "kick it" spot. Every unemployed "scrub a dub dub homie" in the neighborhood would congregate at our house like clockwork, chilling and talking about 'hood topics all day long. Of course, they typically chased their groundbreaking conversations with weed and alcohol.

I was annoyed beyond belief! Every time I would make mention of my dissatisfaction with this bull, we would get into a long argument that would drag out for days. It was completely draining and pointless. I believed that because I was the primary breadwinner of the household, I shouldn't have to bring home the bacon *and* cook it; Justin needed to contribute by doing something other than chilling all day. Resentment began to settle in my spirit.

I don't want to paint the picture that Justin was happy about being unemployed; he was miserable, and his ego was rightly bruised. As a result, he allowed the enemy to make him depressed. That took away his fight, faith and energy to look for work right away. Then, bad habits started to form. After I had complained enough about his homies being at our house, he stopped the practice of having everyone come to the house. However, when he put this annoying habit down, he picked another one up: he started again with his peeping addiction. I was *very* concerned.

Since we had moved into the new house and Justin was unemployed, we enrolled Sierra at the local high school in our new city of residence. Justin was responsible for picking up Kennedy and Sierra from school, because I was working both early and extended hours, trying to make ends meet. I was comfortable with this arrangement, because I thought we had addressed his peeping tendencies; since our move from our dream home, I had not seen or expected the peeping to happen again. Sierra was also okay with the pick-up arrangement; she'd also thought the peeping situation was over. Besides that, she had her little sister with her, so she had no problem with Justin picking them up from school.

For a few months, things seemed to be stable; the constant stream of visitors had ended, and Justin was consistent with dropping the girls off and picking them up after school. Between these drop-offs and pick-ups, he was at home for hours by himself. However, instead of surfing the internet for job leads, he was on the porn sites. It got so bad that our computer crashed due to all of the viruses it had accumulated from his downloads of explicit material.

What really bothered me was when Justin crossed the line and asked to borrow Sierra's computer – the one she uses for her school work. Just as I expected, he watched porn on her computer and forgot to erase the browser history. I confronted him with what he'd done, and he began to yell and cuss me out as if I was the one who had crossed the line! He was hollering and screaming that he was a grown-ass man, and he could do whatever he pleased.

Life was starting to suffocate me. I always felt tired and run down, and I looked a mess. I was working overtime frequently just to make ends meet. My husband was unemployed, unmotivated, and picking up bad habits, and my worst nightmare was becoming a reality: he was having the urge to peep again. He confided in me about his urges.

You, the reader, are probably saying, *She's dumb, she's weak, and she's such a pushover!* I agree. Looking back, I can say that you are correct with all these perceptions, and more. At the time, however, I sincerely thought that I was doing the right thing by preserving my family. I thought that by sticking together, we were showing everyone that we were okay; we had relationship problems just like everyone else, but we were true to our vows, and we would push through. Only now, in retrospect, do I realize that we were only strengthening our façade of our marriage and family. We were just two broken people trying to raise and provide for our kids.

During that time, I honestly thought we were doing what God wanted us to do. However, neither of us consistently took our troubles to God. If things were bearable, we went along with life. When things got hard, we would pray for a day or two, and then we would go back to doing things in our own power, not in the power of the Holy Spirit. You see, there's a difference.

I started to have the strange feeling that Justin had started to peep again, although I still had not seen or heard any evidence to affirm my gut feeling. I just had that annoying feeling in the pit of my stomach that something had changed. Justin began to act very distant – more so than usual – and was very defensive about everything. Then, I got the worst news ever. Not only was Justin still out of work and still having peeping urges, but I found out that his kids' mother was moving onto our street – into Justin's parents' house!

As soon as I heard the news, I thought, *What the hell? Why would my in-laws agree to such a messy situation?* This seemed to be an episode straight out of a Maury Povich-Jerry Springer marathon! It was not a secret that this woman had not been jumping for joy when Justin and I had gotten married. I *still* took issue with the fact that she and Justin had spoken on our honeymoon. Further, no matter how much I contributed to her kids' needs, she was not appreciative of it.

As a woman, I get it. I was the one who married her kids' father. I'd never expected to be her best friend. However, I was at least hoping for us to show some mutual respect towards one another, because I love the kids, too. However, the way that things had gone since Justin and I were married helped me to see that this ideal, respectful relationship that I'd desired to see form between us was probably not going to be an option. I knew that she didn't like me. So, here is my question: If she felt that way, why would she think it was a good idea to move three houses down from us in the first place?

From that day forward, my in-laws and I hardly spoke. I was mad at them for allowing it and pissed at Justin just because. The only thing that made any part of the situation bearable was that I was not complaining about the kids' mother's move to our street by myself; Justin was miserable, too. He'd actually gotten into a huge argument with both his parents and his kids' mother due to her new living arrangement. Although I wanted to move far away from this uncomfortable situation, due to Justin's unsteady income, I did not have enough money or resources to do so. This pissed me off even more, because I felt stuck.

Michelle, Kennedy's godmother, was in my corner during this rough season. She only lived two blocks away, so it was very convenient for her and I to catch up and debrief. I would vent weekly about the shenanigans that had happened on the block. It seemed like every other month, the cops were called by either Justin's parents or his kids' mother regarding a dispute or recent altercation that we'd had.

Again, I was mentally drained. At this time, Sierra was 16, and Kennedy was now six years old. Sierra's attitude was feisty, and at times, disrespectful. I could easily have blamed it on puberty, but I knew better. We still had our random check-ins; however, with me working long and extended hours, our check-ins did not occur as regularly as they had before.

When we did have one of our check-ins around this time, Sierra expressed to me during one of our discussions that she believed that Justin was peeping again, or, as she called it, "Doing that weird stuff again." She said she'd caught him in the backyard looking into her room on a couple of occasions, and he would play it off as if he was looking for something. She thought it was pretty remarkable that he always lost an object when she was changing. I did not share this with Sierra, but I had seen him slowly walk by the bathroom when she was showering, as if he was trying to look through the crack of the door. When I asked what he was doing, he played it off and felt around the frame of the door as if he was intentionally investigating the framework and construction of the door. *A regular Bob the Builder*, I thought.

I had grown accustomed to making smart remarks and comments out loud.

"Funny, it seems like you're only concerned about the door frame work when Sierra is in the bathroom," I would say.

He would complain that I was tripping and walk out the house. I could tell that his urges were becoming harder and harder to control. As far as I know, he stopped peeping at our house and started to peep in the neighborhood.

Because I was no longer close to my in-laws, I literally felt that I had no one to turn to. I still could not tell Mia and Scharae. Charlie had recently married, and I considered myself to be a role model wife to her, so I could not let my truth out. Roxy was going through her own divorce and facing her own personal storms, so I didn't want to dump my issues on top of her own. All of my girlfriends were very aware of Justin's cheating.

Michelle was the only one to whom I really talked about things. She knew a lot about the situation first-hand, because we would share a glass of wine and I would pour out my soul to her. However, I was always very careful not to disclose too much.

No one could know about the peeping – absolutely *no one* – except for Sierra. Each time she caught Justin peeping at her, she would come storming into whatever room I was in and sound off. One day, she stormed into my bedroom in a rage.

"Your damn *husband* is looking at me again, and no, I don't want to forgive him anymore! Mom, *why* are we still here? He apologizes after he first lies to you saying that he wasn't looking at me. Then, he tells the truth. *Why* are you so weak? There is no way that my *stepfather* should know what I look like naked! Mom, this is weird. I am *so* uncomfortable!" She continued, "Please, Mom. I have no respect for this pervert. He cannot parent me anymore. If I do something wrong or disrespectful, I will only listen to you. However, if you keep allowing this and you don't put your foot down, *you* won't be able to parent me either," she threatened.

I *clearly* had displaced anger, because I cussed her out in my rage. How dare she give me, her mother, an ultimatum? Did she not hear me yell and cuss at Justin whenever he was caught? Didn't she know that I was already stressed out over this?

The truth is, I was such a selfish, weak girl. I would have had to be in order to bully my kid, who was being victimized, rather than the actual predator who had committed the violation. Ever since Sierra's last blow-up and threatening not to listen to Justin anymore, the tension level in the house was unbearable. Then, the unspeakable happened.

One Saturday evening, Kennedy and I were in the living room watching television, when I heard an outburst of yelling and cussing. To this day, I am not sure what started the mayhem, but Justin had lunged at Sierra and she had lunged back at him. When I ran into the room, I saw him over her, trying to restrain her on her bed. I lost it.

I jumped on Justin's back and hit him in his face. Then, he and I went at it. Funny thing: this whole time that I had been keeping Justin's secrets, my life was about ensuring that Justin was protected, not my daughter. However, when it mattered most, my first instinct was to protect my daughter; in a serious altercation between Justin and my daughter, I jumped to her rescue without a moment's hesitation. I think I shocked myself by tending to Sierra's rather than Justin's needs first; when the altercation abruptly ended, I had bruises on my legs and Justin had a huge gash on his face.

Sierra kept shouting, “I *told* your ass not to parent me! You lost that privilege when you stopped acting like a father figure, you pervert!”

“I'm going to call your damn father! This is my house and I can do as I please!” Justin shouted back in his anger.

“Call him, and I will tell him that you’ve been watching me,” she said with a tone that dared him to make the move.

Justin thought she was bluffing; he thought wrong. He called Nigel. “Can you come over?” Justin asked. “Something happened at the house regarding Sierra, and I would like to talk with you about it.” Nigel agreed to come over.

My world, my façade, started to crumble right before my eyes. This was the *opposite* of quiet and staying down low; in calling Nigel, we had just opened Pandora's Box. This meeting was about to accelerate a ripple effect from the years of hiding. When Justin hung up the phone, I started to yell at him at the top of my lungs.

“What the hell did you do that for? Why did you call him? I *told* you not to parent her! She does not respect you, and you have no right to attempt to parent her when you invade her privacy!”

In his egotistical manner, Justin said, “She's not going to say anything.” He smirked and walked outside to his man cave.

I was dumbfounded. *Is this dude clueless?* I thought. I could not believe that he himself believed that crap. *Of course* she was going to say something. Justin had called her father to discipline her for not respecting him, the very person who had been violating her privacy.

I went into Sierra's room to try and reason with her before Nigel arrived. The moment I walked into the room, she said, “No, Mom. I can't take it anymore. When my dad comes, I’m telling him.”

"Sierra," I said, "what happens in our house is *our* business."

"Well, Mom, that's the problem. Justin knows that all too well. He gets to do what he wants, and he gives us a fake apology. Wait a while, and he goes right back to that weird stuff. For that very reason, no one knows his secrets. I am not hiding anymore. I love you, Mommy, but I am *so* uncomfortable! You've *changed*. It was better when it was just you and me. Kennedy is the only good thing from this. That's all."

"Sierra, Baby, I understand. But we need to—" I began.

Ding dong! The doorbell rang. My heart dropped. Nigel was at the front door. I didn't finish my thought.

"Your dad is here," I said to Sierra.

Sierra eagerly made a beeline for the front door. She was trying to get to her father before Justin had a chance to speak to him. Justin was a master manipulator, and she did not want him to have the opportunity to downplay anything, period.

I slowly walked to the living room. My stomach was in knots, my head was pounding, and I felt a bit light-headed. Just as Sierra had suspected, Justin was the first person to greet Nigel at the door. All four of us stood at the front door awkwardly.

Nigel said, "What's going on?"

I invited him in, and we all sat in the living room. Sierra, Nigel and I sat on the same couch, while Justin sat by himself on the matching loveseat. Before we began, I excused myself to go into my room and check on Kennedy, who was fast asleep on the bed. Walking back into the living room, I felt weak and nervous. I sat back down on the same couch as Sierra and her dad.

Nigel looked at me. “Bree, what's up? Why did I get summoned over here?”

Justin took the lead. “We had an altercation that got physical.” Nigel immediately turned his body in Sierra’s direction, maintaining eye contact as Justin rattled off his version of the scuffle.

Sierra burst out and said, “Dad, the reason why this happened today is that I told him he is not allowed to discipline me anymore.”

Nigel asked, “What do you mean you told your stepfather not to discipline you anymore? Are you kidding me? He is a grown ass man that helps provide for you.” Nigel quickly turned his face to me as if to say, *Are you hearing this bull? Say something!*

I could not even make eye contact with him. I was feeling weaker and weaker by the moment.

Sierra burst out in tears. “Dad, he *watches* me!”

“Watches you? What do you mean?” he asked.

“When I take showers, when I get dressed, all the time! He knows what I look like naked. He's a pervert!” Sierra sobbed.

“What the...!" screamed Nigel. Now, Nigel was standing up looking straight towards Justin. “Has he touched you?” he asked accusingly, not taking his gaze off of Justin.

“No,” she cried.

I started to cry uncontrollably. I stood up to put my body between Justin and Nigel, but I fainted. I blacked out under the stress of Nigel finding out. Our family’s dirty secret coming out was too overwhelming for me.

I came to after a few moments. As I opened my eyes, I saw Nigel and Sierra standing over me. The noise from the commotion must have awakened Kennedy, because Justin now had her on his lap. Nigel helped me up from the ground.

"Bree... Man, how long has this been going on? Why didn't you tell me? That's my *baby*!" he said, pointing over at Sierra who sat on the couch with a strained look on her face.

"I didn't know how to tell anyone," I said wearily. "I prayed about it, and we told our pastor that he had a porn addiction, but I never had the courage to say anything else. Plus, Justin didn't touch her. He just looked," I said.

Nigel looked as if he had to restrain himself from slapping me after I said that. He turned his attention back to Justin.

"Man, this is my *baby*, Nigga! You're supposed to protect her from stuff like this, not *violate* her!" he said, fuming.

"Man... man..." Justin mumbled. "I have a problem. I fantasize about her, but I never touched her! I'm working on my issues. I messed up man, I messed up," he confessed.

"How many times have you done this to my daughter?" Nigel asked.

Before Justin could answer, Sierra called out, "A lot! It started when we first moved into that big house."

Justin continued his defense. "I'm flawed man, just like all people, but I love my family, and I'm trying to work on it."

Nigel just stared at Justin. An awkward silence filled the living room.

Nigel, who also is a man of God, said, "If you're working on it, so be it, but I agree with my baby. Do not parent her. Not at all. You're sending her mixed messages. Her mom and I will deal with any issues she may have. You've lost those privileges."

Nigel turned to me. "Bree," he said, speaking in an authoritative tone.

"Yes?" I responded.

"You and I need to talk. He is your husband, the head of your household, but this is some *bull*!"

"I agree."

"I won't tell you what to do with your marriage; that's not my business. But *she* needs to be protected, and you need to keep me in the loop. Completely! Understood?" he demanded.

"I understand," I responded. We ended the meeting with a prayer. Nigel told Sierra to get dressed; he wanted to spend the day with her and get her out of the environment. Sierra happily got dressed, kissed me and Kennedy, and left for the day with her dad.

I felt like a weight had been lifted from me. *Okay, her dad knows. I am not in hiding anymore now. Justin has to get his act together, and we are going to be okay,* I thought. I was still furious with Justin, but I was relieved that I now had an ally in Sierra's father.

Nigel and I, for the most part, get along well. We were young when Sierra came into our lives, but we always had a good friendship that had weathered well, considering how young and stubborn we both were. I also knew that Sierra was going to give her father an earful about the peeping and the masturbation conversation that Justin had initiated with her when she was younger. I was not looking forward to our talk, but I knew that it was necessary, and I was going to be truthful. He knew the worst part already, and he had also heard the gossip around the city about the countless women with whom Justin had had affairs.

Sierra and Nigel came back later that night. Sierra had such a look of relief on her face; I could literally see that she felt protected and vindicated.

Nigel and I went onto my front porch and started talking. I apologized again for not being honest with him and promised that it wouldn't happen again. Just as I'd suspected, Sierra had divulged everything. Nigel had been updated about our entire situation.

"Nigel," I said, "if he would have touched her, we would not still be here."

"If he had touched her, I would have a case against him," Nigel replied. I nodded my head in agreement. He reiterated the need for me to keep him posted and to regularly touch base with him about Sierra.

"Of course," I responded. Nigel knew that I was not the kind of woman that would call him all of the time about our daughter. I am savvy, and I can figure things out by myself. Also, Nigel had recently married for the second time, and I respected that. I knew his wife from the past. She and I had gotten along well, because I could see her genuine love for our daughter.

The morning following the altercation, Justin apologized once again to me and Sierra for the incident. By this time, I was growing tired of hearing him say, "I'm sorry."

To Justin's apology, Sierra replied, "Okay, but my dad agreed. You are not allowed to parent me, so please don't. My parents together will handle that." She walked proudly out of the room. Justin didn't say a word.

I decided to be proactive about the situation. I tried everything. I got up and went to the linen store to purchase blackout curtains for the girls' room. I was trying to do anything that would minimize Justin's opportunities to peep at Sierra. I also made sure that I had a lot of sex with Justin so that he wouldn't feel that he was lacking any sexual attention. Notice that I said "sex," not "love making." There was no intimate, emotional connection for me when we slept together. I was simply trying to resolve a problem.

I was miserable, and so was Justin, but we needed to keep this sham of a marriage going, so we did what we had to do. We'd been together for six years now. We'd invested all of this time and energy and all of these emotions, so we couldn't stop now; we were in too deep. Plus, Nigel knew about Justin's issue now, so some of the guilt was lifted off of my conscience.

For the next four to five months, I felt like I was on autopilot. I was working overtime, and Justin was still out of work. I was dealing with him staying out all night. Only God knows what he was doing while he was out; he could have been keeping company with our neighbors, cheating with other women, or hanging out with bad company.

In the midst of all this, Sierra became ill, and I needed money for her to have a procedure. I did not have it, so I called Nigel, who also did not have it. We became frustrated with one another, both of us having our own feelings about Sierra and having strong opinions on who could handle it better. We started lashing out at one another verbally over the phone.

I believe that this was clearly the work of the enemy; he saw the alliance that Nigel and I had formed and sought to cause a huge rift in our unity. When truth is revealed in the light, it takes away the power that the enemy has over you, because you no longer have to keep the lie going in darkness; the enemy needs darkness in order to hide things.

After the truth was revealed about Justin's issue and Nigel and I no longer had to hide it from him, the enemy was mad! He devised a plan to split apart our unified front, and Nigel and I both fell into the enemy's trap, hook, line and sinker. We started a war – a *full-fledged* war – against each other.

Sierra's medical procedure was taken care of; thankfully, between me and my dad, we were able to pay to get it done. However, Nigel and I were now enemies. Everything that we'd told him in confidence, he told to others. However, what got back to me was not that he'd said Justin was peeping. It was now rumored that Justin was having sex with or touching my daughter, which was a lie.

It got so bad that Nigel took us to court to petition for full custody of Sierra. I was not going to let that happen. Sierra had always lived with me, and I'd never denied Nigel access to his daughter. However, because of the horrendous accusations of sexual abuse that Nigel had made against us, Child Protective Services made a surprise visit to my home and interviewed both of my kids, saying that they'd received an anonymous tip. Thankfully, the agent did not see any signs of physical or sexual abuse and closed the case.

Sierra was hurt that her father and mother's relationship was now strained. She felt torn. She loved her dad, but she didn't want to live with him, so when Child Protective Services paid a visit, she did everything she could to ensure that she and Kennedy were not removed from our home. She was confused about why their documents said that she had been touched.

After Child Protective Services were sent to my home to investigate, my feelings were hurt, and my pride as a woman and a mother were bruised. I did what any pissed off single mother would do: in my rage, I brought child support charges against Nigel. The *real* battle had begun.

We were summoned to appear in court, and the process was brutal. The morning of our first court hearing, I was a mess. I kept thinking, *Why embellish the truth? Say what you were told about the peeping. Sierra doesn't say she's been touched, so the court isn't going to have a problem with it.*

We all went in to see the judge, who told us that this was an informal hearing. He said that we would need to have a court date when the case would be presented. We were ushered downstairs to see his court clerk, and we were told that she would process the paperwork and advise us of the official court date. When we got to the clerk's office, I saw Nigel laughing and playing with the woman behind the desk. She had our court documents in her hand. *Why*? Lo and behold, this woman was not only the court clerk, this was one of Nigel's homegirls. I was pissed.

I could tell that Nigel had made a comment about me because she looked at me while he was talking to her. I was super ready to clown or go off if she was not professional. I mean, my guard was up, and my guns were locked and loaded. I had that "I wish a Nigga *would"* mentality!

She called my case number. I took a deep breath and walked forward toward her, confidently and professionally.

"Good morning," she said with a smile. I want to say it was fake because it was the same smile she gave to everyone who approached her desk.

"Morning," I mumbled back.

She was a petite, brown-complexioned woman. I mean, she was cute or whatever. I have to admit that although I had concerns at first, our interaction was professional. I could tell that she did not play with her job. Even though she clearly had a friendship with Nigel, she did not treat me any differently than anyone else, and I respected that. I glanced at her name on the desk name plate. It said "Tiny."

I left the court feeling stressed and sad that my years of friendship with Nigel were now broken.

My façade was back on, and now, it was back even stronger. Looking back on those times, I should have received both an

Emmy and an Oscar for my stellar performances. As a family, we were back in church, had fun date nights and family outings – anything to prove naysayers wrong! However, although I was smiling on the outside, I was deteriorating on the inside.

Our family seemed to be running pretty normally, for the most part, for at least the next year to a year-and-a-half. Unfortunately, Justin's kids' mother was still living down the street, and we had what felt like weekly encounters with that drama. I started to grow used to drama. It was my new normal. I became desensitized to it and felt numb when it occurred. In fact, I actually expected and welcomed drama into my life. It had a permanent address that seemed to be attached to me, and I was growing more comfortable with it by the day.

Throughout all of the constant drama, Mia, Scharae and I still had our morning conference calls each day. When Mia had heard that Nigel was taking me to court, she was hot! Remember, Mia is fiery and she is loyal. She doesn't like bully tactics. She had a conversation with Nigel through direct messages on social media, and after she'd said her piece, she immediately deleted him as a friend. Roxy did the same, minus the conversation. I was torn because she knew us both. Part of me felt like my drama had cost her a friend.

Scharae took a different approach. She, for the most part, remained neutral and silent throughout the drama. Her main concern was Sierra; she wanted to make sure that Sierra was good. For me, it was the same; my main concern was making sure that Sierra was okay. Both Scharae and Mia are also very guarded as it pertains to Sierra. They're both her godmothers, and they take the title very seriously, even to this day.

What added fuel to the fire of the drama was that both Justin and Nigel were equally popular in our small city, so the rumors had exploded. It felt like the city was divided with people being on one side or the other; they either supported and believed Nigel or they supported and believed Justin. However, no one knew the complete truth outside of Nigel, Sierra, Justin and me.

Thankfully, in the end, we ended up not having to go to court; Nigel set his pride aside – pride was the problem for every one of us involved in the situation – and cancelled his petition for full custody of Sierra; he didn't want to drag our daughter through a messy court case. I set aside my own pride, immediately agreed with his decision, and the case was dropped. However, our friendship had been broken.

Caught in the middle was Sierra. Throughout the battle, she felt that she had to pick a side, and she'd picked me, her mom. I felt bad that she'd even felt she had to choose one of her parents or the other. I felt so bad; not only had my own drama affected my daughter, but it had now affected her relationship with her dad.

At this time, I did not have an intimate relationship with the Lord, only a superficial one. Whenever I got in trouble, I called on Him. I was a "crisis Christian." My flesh was always in control of my life, meaning that the enemy was still guiding me through his influence. I was not awakened to what it truly meant to have a close walk with God. However, even through all of the bad mistakes and decisions I made, God, in His mercy, still covered me with His grace.

Sometimes, I think back on all that could have happened during that dramatic season of my life, things that God prevented from happening. I could have lost my daughter's love and trust. I could have gone to court for the allegations of keeping my daughter in an environment where she was sexually abused. I could have lost my life when I contemplated and prepared myself to commit suicide. I could have lost the sisterhood of all my friends, including Mia, Scharae, Roxy, Michelle, Charlie, Tiffany and Angel. I could have lost both of my kids after Child Protective Services came to my home for their investigation. And the worst thought of all: Justin could have done more than just peep at Sierra; he could have touched her. God would not let any of these things be. Instead, in God we receive new mercies daily, and that's exactly what He gave to me during this critical period of my life. For this alone, I shout for joy!

During the choppy period with Nigel, my relationship with Scharae felt strained. She and I talked, but we hardly saw one another, even though we both lived in the same city. Fortunately, no love was lost; we just went through a hard time, but we are still like sisters. I believe that Scharae had probably detected that I was not being a 100% honest about everything that was going on in my life. Although she never voiced this, it was something that I sensed. Needless to say, throughout the dramatic years of my life, we missed out on making some significant memories and celebrating some big milestones because of the emotional rather than the physical distance between us.

Mia had flown in about four times within that two-year time frame. When she came into town, she, Scharae and I would all meet up. When the three of us hung out, it was like the old times; we always had a blast together! Pretty soon, the three of us would have another reason to get together again. Scharae was about to celebrate a huge milestone: she was turning 40! Scharae was throwing a big black-and-white themed birthday party, and Mia and I were not going to miss it!

We all were excited about the big event, because Scharae *really* knows how to throw a party! Best of all, the three of us were going to be together again to add on to our many memories and milestones that we'd celebrated together. Further, Scharae is a social butterfly, so everyone in our city was aware of her upcoming party. We were looking forward to seeing all of our old friends and acquaintances who would be there.

I was hoping and praying that Justin would not want to go with me to the party. By this time, I was over him; the tension of our marriage left it hanging by one last thread. We didn't talk anymore. I'd stopped having sex with him. We were basically roommates. I was also aware that he was still dealing with different women. Every time I walked into the room, he was either hanging up his phone or texting. Guess what? I didn't care. I didn't give a bleep *at all*! Truth be told, I was actually okay that someone else was doing him, because I didn't want to anymore.

I was done with living the façade. It was over. I was completely done with Justin. As a matter of fact, Sierra was at the point of blurting out everything, disclosing all of our family's business to the world, and I didn't even care anymore. It was too much energy to hide and cover-up all of the secrets and lies. No more façade!

eight

The Party

On the day of Scharae's 40th birthday party, she and I headed out first thing in the morning to prepare. We had a lot of errands to run, plus we were going to pick up Mia from the airport. The party was being held at a local hotel, so Mia and I had booked a room to share so that we could enjoy ourselves to the fullest.

Since I was not going to be home that night, I'd already made arrangements for Sierra and Kennedy to spend the night at Michelle's house; once I'd discovered that Justin had a peeping problem, I always made sure that if I was going out of town or staying out late, the girls would spend the night out. The anxiety of "what if" always plagued my mind, so I always planned ahead.

Just before I left the house that morning, I went into the girls' room while they were still fast asleep. I woke Sierra gently. She slowly opened her big, beautiful almond-shaped eyes.

"Yes, Mom?"

"Hey, Babe," I said. "I'm leaving now. I'll be back later. Call me if you need anything, and remember you are going to Auntie Michelle's tonight."

"Okay, Mama. Tell my aunties I said 'Hi' and I love them," she replied in a small, sleepy voice.

"Will do!" I said, leaving the room.

Justin was in the kitchen making himself a cup of coffee. He and I had not really spoken in weeks, and we had not been sexually intimate for a while.

I mumbled, "I'm leaving."

He walked out of the kitchen to where I was.

"What did you say?" I rolled my eyes in irritation. *Clearly* he had heard me; he was just trying to make a power move.

I stopped walking, turned around to face him, and said, "I-am-leav-ing." I purposely over-pronounced every flipping syllable in the sentence so he would have no reason to pretend that he hadn't heard me this time.

"Oh," he responded.

I grabbed my phone and texted Scharae and then walked out of the door. When I jumped into the car with Scharae, she could tell by my demeanor that I was a bit irritated.

"What's wrong?" she asked.

"Nothing, girl," I said. I played down my irritation, not wanting to ruin her day.

"Is he coming tonight?" she asked. I gave her a look that said, *Hell no*!

"I don't think so," I said, "but you know him. He just pops up at the darndest times. He knows that I'm staying over, and I purposely didn't get my own room so that he wouldn't get any ideas about trying to visit my room in the middle of the night." We both chuckled. Then, we hit the freeway on our way to LAX to pick up our sister Mia. I felt 21 again!

Both Scharae and I texted and phoned the people we knew about her black and white party, and we also put out posts about the party on social media. In the midst of sending out and responding to the many messages and posts, Scharae's phone went dead. She was the birthday girl, so there were a lot of last minute questions about the party and "Happy birthday" messages. The overflow of activity had caused her battery to die, so of course, her people started calling my phone trying to reach her.

We pulled up to the curbside at the LAX passenger pickup location and saw Mia standing there with her bags, watching for us. As we pulled closer towards her, we could tell by her expression that she was bit upset. We were a little late, and every time she'd tried to reach either of us, she'd gotten our voicemails.

"Hey, girl!" Scharae and I both sang in unison, as if we were members of the harmonizing girls group En Vogue.

"You're late!" was all that Mia shot back in response as she opened the car door.

We all started laughing because we knew that even though she was aggravated, she was happy to see us. Mia jumped into the back seat of the car with her bag, and we took off.

"So, what's on the agenda?" asked Mia. I rolled my eyes. She was also so into logistics!

"Damn, girl! You just *got* to Cali. Just *roll*!" I replied, encouraging her to relax for a moment and enjoy the ride.

"You are not my mama, so you can refrain from the scolding!" she said.

My relationship with Mia has a lot of love, but it's also extremely low-key argumentative. She bugs me to my core, and I know that sometimes, I bug her, too.

Scharae, who is usually the peacemaker of the three of us, responded to Mia.

"We pre-made our appointments, so we are on our way there now. Period," she said, trying to put an end to my and Mia's exchange.

I shook my head in agreement. Like me, Scharae knows that every time we all hook up, we always get our nails done. That's why, to me, Mia's question was a stupid one.

"Not today, Devil!" I said out loud. Again, we all started to laugh uncontrollably.

Off we went to our nail appointment. Afterwards, we enjoyed a lunch date, and then we completed our errands in preparation for the night's shindig. We headed back to my house around 4 p.m. I still needed to pack my overnight bag and make sure that Kennedy and Sierra had made it off to Michelle's house before I left for the night.

We pulled up to my house, and I could see that Justin was still at home; his car was parked in the driveway. When we walked into the house, Scharae and Mia made a beeline to the girls' room. As I headed to my room, I heard Sierra's and Kennedy's cheerful voices.

"Aunties!" they both shouted. Although I could not see them, I'm sure that there were lots of hugs and kisses.

Justin was there as I walked into our room.

"Are Scharae and Mia here?" he asked.

"Yes," I replied. Justin liked my girlfriends, but he'd always seemed to have an attitude whenever we were all together.

I got some clothes together, pulled out my overnight bag, and began to pack as he watched me.

"Are you coming to the party tonight?" I asked out of curiosity. In my head, I was thinking, *Please say no! Please say no!* He simply shrugged his shoulders as if to suggest that I had asked a silly question.

"Not sure. Why? Are you going to have your boyfriend there trying to agitate me?" he asked.

"No!" I said, laughing. "Did your side chicks get the memo not to approach me?" I asked as I walked out of the room.

Sierra was sitting in the living room when I walked out of the bedroom. Kennedy also came out of her bedroom, excited to see everyone. Scharae and Mia also sat in the living room. I began getting the girls ready to leave.

"Mom, are you going to be here for a bit? For a while longer?" Sierra asked.

"Why?" I asked.

"Do I have time to take a quick shower?" she asked. I looked at Sierra and nodded my head. I knew that she had been waiting for me to come home first.

As I was doing Kennedy's hair, out of my peripheral vision, I could see Mia looking at me. I turned to look at her, and we made eye contact.

"She's been here all day waiting for you to be here to take a *shower*?" Mia murmured in a low voice. I did what I do best: I ignored it and pretended like I hadn't heard a thing.

Within 20 minutes, Sierra was showered, dressed, and ready to go. She gathered her and Kennedy's bags and called her Auntie Michelle, letting her know that she and her sister were on their way. Sierra had her own car by this time. She kissed me and her aunties and then left. Fifteen minutes after my girls left, I was ready to go, too.

"See you in the morning," I yelled to Justin from the living room as Scharae, Mia and I walked out the door.

As soon as we got to the car, Scharae's first question was, "Why did my God baby wait until mid-day to take a shower when you returned home?"

"Maybe she's lazy," I answered. "Or better yet, maybe you should ask your God baby yourself!"

"Maybe we *will* do exactly that," replied Mia.

"Do *what*?" I asked. I quickly changed the subject.

On our way to the hotel, we stopped to pick up Destiny, a friend who is like a big sister to all of us. Destiny was always there to listen, and she was a great big sister. Always the voice of reason, she often played referee when the three of us would occasionally get into an argument.

Off we all went to our hotel. Everyone was fired up super excited about the birthday party, which was to begin in just a few short hours.

As soon as we got to the hotel, we all shared a birthday celebration toast, clinking our glasses in recognition of Scharae's big 40-year milestone. Then, Destiny and I went downstairs to check on Scharae's party decorations. After also making sure that the DJ and photographer were on point, we went to our hotel rooms to get our outfits together.

Scharae's 40th year black and white party was fabulous, and Scharae looked *stunning*! She was the "hostess with the mostest" and made her rounds to greet each one of her guests. Everyone was having a blast, taking pictures, catching up on old times, and grooving on the dance floor all night long.

When Michelle made it to the party, she saw me grooving on the dance floor and made her way towards me.

"Is Justin here yet?" she asked, raising her voice so that I could hear her over the music.

"Yet?" I asked. "Wait... *what*?" I didn't realize that he was going to be coming to the party.

"Yeah. He just sent me a text and said he was on his way," she said. She'd assumed that he was already there.

I got off the dance floor to collect my thoughts. I was pissed that Justin was going to come and possibly ruin my good time. It took way too much energy to put up the front that we were still good as a couple, energy that I didn't have tonight.

Before long, Justin did arrive. As he walked in, I watched as he was greeted by Roxy. She was now divorced, but she had been dating a wonderful man, who was a former schoolmate (and whom she would go on to marry in the future). Roxy looked so disgustingly happy these days, and I was so happy that my friend was smiling again. She gave Justin a warm hug. She genuinely cares for him, and they truly had a bond.

Justin tried a few times to interact with me, but I was not interested. It didn't take long for him to pick up on the hint that I was not thrilled that he had come.

"I'm leaving," he said.

"Okay," was all that I replied to him.

On his way out, Michelle stopped him. She asked him if he was leaving, and he said that he was. She told him to hold on a second, because she'd had a headache and had decided to call it a night herself. Michelle came and said goodbye to me, letting me know that Justin was going to walk her to her car, period. I gave her a hug and a kiss, and they both left. I was sad that Michelle had left, but I was relieved that Justin had gotten the hint and had excused himself.

"Where did Justin go?" Mia asked.

"Back home, or wherever," I responded. She knew what I meant by that.

We resumed partying again, getting back on the dance floor and having a ball. After a few minutes, we were partying so hard that I accidentally bumped into another lady on the dance floor. When I turned around to apologize to her, I did a double take; her face looked so familiar. I realized that it was the court clerk, Tiny. She looked at me and I looked at her.

"Do you work at the court?" I asked.

"Yes, I do," she replied, smiling. "Nigel's daughter's mother, yes?" she asked.

"Tiny, right?" I replied.

"Yeah, that's my name," she said.

"Do you know my best friend, Scharae?" I asked.

"Yes! That's my sis!" she said.

"Huh?"

"That's my Boo! We go to church together," she said.

"Wow, what a small world!" I said. "Nice to meet you outside of the drama," I said, extending my hand to shake hers.

However, Tiny said, "If you're one of Scharae's friends, you *have* to be cool!" and she gave me a hug instead. Although I had no idea of it at the time, this would be the start of a beautiful friendship.

We continued enjoying ourselves, dancing, laughing, and celebrating. The party ended around 2 a.m. By that time, I was exhausted and the hotel bed was calling my name.

I slept like a baby and woke up rested. After Mia and I were both awake, we recapped the party, discussing the highlights and all the funny things that had happened the previous evening.

Our room phone rang. It was Scharae.

"You ladies up for getting breakfast?" she asked.

"Yes," we both eagerly replied. We were starving! I'd had a bit too much to drink the night before. I was not hung over; I just needed to refuel with a hearty breakfast. We agreed to meet downstairs within the hour.

We showered and headed down to the hotel restaurant. Every moment that we spent during this time was special, because Mia would be leaving for the airport within the next four hours.

During breakfast, I received a phone call from Sierra.

"Mom, I can't take it anymore. I can't keep this front up! Everyone likes and respects Justin, but they really don't know what kind of man he truly is. It's getting on my last nerve!" she said, sounding frustrated.

Because I was at the breakfast table with Scharae and Mia I said, "We'll talk later."

"No, Mom, we won't!" She hung up the phone.

"Is everything okay?" Scharae and Mia both asked, sensing my concern.

"Yes, it's all good. Sierra is just an emotional wreck. When will *puberty* be over?" I replied jokingly.

Before I could say another word, Justin called. As soon as I answered the phone, he began yelling. Although Scharae and Mia could not make out his words, they could tell that he was pissed off and that something was wrong.

Apparently, Sierra had been disrespectful to him at church, and he did not like it. He told me I'd better get a hold of my kid, because he wasn't out for the disrespect. Again, I could not make a rebuttal, because I was at the breakfast table. Just as I'd done with Sierra, I told him that we would talk later.

When my breakfast arrived, I didn't touch it; my appetite was ruined, and my nerves were once again bad. After the girls ate, all three of us headed back to our room so Mia could start to pack for her flight home. As we made our way back to our room, although the three of us were together, I felt sad and alone. It was easy for me not to harp on my secret situation when I was at home, but when I was with my sisters, the fact that I was hiding something so big from them made me feel lonely and isolated in their midst.

I remember what happened next like it was yesterday. We got to my and Mia's room, and Scharae was lying across Mia's bed. I was sitting on the edge of my own bed, and Mia was on the floor with her suitcase open, packing her clothes. Everything was moving in slow motion.

I was usually really good at fighting the urge to tell my sisters about what was going on at home. After all, I had been hiding it for years. However, as I sat there with them in the room, I heard a voice that said, "Tell them. Tell them *now*!" I must have repeated the words out loud because both Mia and Scharae turned and looked at me, confused.

"What do you mean now, Bree?" Scharae asked.

Before I could stop myself, I blurted it out.

"Justin is a Peeping Tom, and he looked at Sierra! I can't take it anymore!" I burst into tears.

Their questions came flying at me. I wasn't sure who was asking what. Emotions were instantly heightened upon hearing the earth-shattering news I'd just shared.

"What the *hell* do you mean, 'peeping at Sierra?' How long has this been happening? Why didn't you tell us? Wait a minute... this makes *sense* now. Yesterday, we were wondering why she waited the entire day to take a damn shower. She didn't feel comfortable taking a shower without you there! Has he touched her?"

The questions came nonstop, and I was in no position to answer them. I was bawling and feeling ashamed, embarrassed, and totally overwhelmed. Mia was angry at Justin and the situation. She was about to blow her lid. Scharae was angry and sad, but level-headed. I just sat on the bed crying a pool of tears that seemed like they wouldn't stop. However, the secret was finally out; I had finally shared the secret that I had been holding on to and hiding from my dearest sisters for years. With every second that passed in that hotel room, I could actually feel the burden being lifted. I felt lighter. I could breathe more freely. My tears began to subside.

"It's out now," I said. "It was *killing* me keeping it from you guys!"

"So, Nigel was right with his allegations?" Mia asked.

"No," I answered. "What it said in the court papers was that she was physically getting touched. That part wasn't true."

"What made you tell us?" Scharae asked.

"I was feeling anxious, and something made me do it," I answered.

The statement "something made me do it" was incorrect. It was not "something," it was Someone. The Holy Spirit had released me from my own prison. The provision was made, and the healing process had finally begun. Nothing is a coincidence; everything happens in God's perfect time. You see, this was not a conversation to be had during one of our daily phone conferences. God had orchestrated our lives, by the Holy Spirit, so that we would be in this exact place and in this exact moment in order for me to release.

I began to cry again, and Mia hugged me. I could see that she was fighting back her own tears. This was no time for her to be sad; she was way too angry.

"My poor baby," Mia and Scharae both said.

As Mia finished packing, I began to divulge more information about the inappropriate talks Justin had had with Sierra, the shower incident, and the continued peeping. The more I released, the more things began to seem clearer to me.

"He has to go," I said. "He can't spend another night in our home."

"He's a predator. Period!" Scharae said. Then, she asked, "So that stuff I heard around the city was true?"

I looked at her. "What stuff?"

"I heard a long time ago about some peeping stuff. I thought it was just hood talk, but now it seems there was some truth in it," she explained.

I had a flashback to when the petite firecracker parole lady had warned me about Justin and how I had looked at her as if she had the plague. I began to bawl.

For some reason, in that moment, I felt all of Sierra's fears and how uncomfortable she must have felt over the years, especially since my first reaction was to keep everything under wraps in order to protect my marriage. Thoughts about how I had treated my precious daughter flooded my mind. *What kind of woman am I? How can I expect my daughter to be braver than me? She should hate me – surely, not trust me – but she doesn't. She adores me and still allows me the opportunity to mother her, even though I've been wrong.*

If God were to make the decision to not extend to me any more grace for the rest of my life, I couldn't complain. By His grace, He had already spared my daughter's love for me despite all that I'd put her through, and for that I will be forever grateful.

In that hotel room with my two sisters, the release period of my life finally began. I was no longer held captive to the secrets that had imprisoned me in the darkness for so long.

The ride to the airport was an emotional one. As we made our way there to drop Mia off, Justin called to ask when I would be home.

"Justin, it's over. The secret is out," I said, still feeling the lightness of my release.

"What are you talking about, Bree?" he asked.

"I told Scharae and Mia. They know about the peeping, about you peeping on Sierra, everything."

"What are you doing!" he shouted. "Are you alone?"

"No, they're here with me now," I said. Silence filled both the car and the space on the other end of the phone. "You have to move out today... TODAY!" I continued. "You can no longer stay in my home after you've continuously disrespected Sierra's privacy. I'm on my way home, so please start packing now. I'll talk with the girls later tonight. I don't want them to see you."

"But Baby, I love you!" he pleaded.

"That may be true, but with the peeping and the cheating, we need to separate," I said sternly.

"Where would I go?" he asked.

"I'm not sure, but I have to look out for the girls' best interest."

"If I leave, we can't fix it." He was trying to manipulate me.

"We've been together all this time, and you haven't fixed it. You need help from a professional. I can't take on this task anymore. It's costing me my sanity," I said.

"I love you, Bree."

"I believe you do, but I have to love me and the girls more. I've done it your way for years and we've made no progress. Just agree to leave and move out." I thanked him for his cooperation, and I hung the phone up.

We pulled up to the airport.

"You made the right decision. Justin is a grown man, and your babies need you to protect them," Mia said as we pulled up to the airport. I cried like a baby when she got out the car. We embraced, and she said, "You're going to be all right." Then, still fighting back her tears from falling, she looked at Scharae and said, "Sister, take care of her!"

"Of course!" Scharae responded. "We're sisters. We will get through it!"

As we pulled off from the airport, I was emotionally drained. Who would have thought that my whole world would be turned upside down that morning? On the way home, Scharae prayed with me and assured me that everything would be okay. *This, too, shall pass.*

nine

Seek

I felt anxious the whole way home. Justin had called me a few times asking to talk. I told him that when I got home, we could talk briefly, but he still had to pack his stuff and leave – no exceptions. He'd agreed to leave, but he wanted to speak with me first. I agreed to a short meeting; I did not want him to have enough time to talk me out of my decision. I also needed the time to have a conversation with Sierra and Kennedy, as this would definitely be shocking news for both of them.

When Scharae and I pulled up, Justin's car was in the driveway. I could see that he had already begun the packing process; the back door of the car was open, and there was a suitcase and a duffle bag sitting in the open trunk.

"You want me to come in with you, Sister?" Scharae asked as I gathered my things to exit the car. She clearly sounded ready for whatever. "I never sleep!" she said, implying that she had her boxing gloves on, and she was ready to fight, if need be.

“Relax, Mohammad!” I chuckled. “I got this. I think it’s best if you don't wait around. I promise I’ll call you when he leaves.”

“You’d better! Matter of fact, if I don't hear from you in like, the next three hours, I'm rolling back over here!”

“Four hours,” I corrected. I wasn’t sure how long our conversation was going to take, but four hours seemed like a sufficient amount of time to say what we needed to say. I wanted to have time to make him feel the hurt of being separated from our family, and we still had to discuss how we were going to handle dealing with Kennedy.

“Fine. Four hours. I’ll call you, and if you don't pick up, I am coming over!”

“Cool,” I said. She gave me a hug and said, “Put your big girl panties on and stand your ground. He has to leave. The girls take precedence, and his reign is *over*!”

I agreed. “Yes, it's about the girls and I first.” I got my bags from Scharae’s car and headed towards the house.

When I walked into the house, Justin was in our room. He was looking through the closet and in his dresser drawers. His eyes looked red, as if he'd been crying.

“Hey,” I said.

Justin looked at me without uttering a word. For about 30 seconds, he just glared at me with an expression of betrayal on his face, as if to ask, *How dare you tell our secret?* The reason that I was so familiar with this particular expression was because it was one that I wore daily.

“I thought you said you loved me and you wanted to help me?” he began.

"I *do* love you, Justin, but I can't help you. You need professional help. I need to protect my girls, and buying blackout curtains is not enough. Keeping the girls at home with me is not enough. Trying to protect them from you is actually tiring and counterproductive."

"Bree, if I leave, you won't want me back. You'll want a divorce down the line."

"No one said 'divorce,' Justin. I said you need help, but you can't do it here. I need space right now. I have to prove to Sierra that she matters. For so many years, your feelings were the only ones I considered, and she had to go along with it because I said so. But she's hurting, not just from you, but from me, because I did nothing to fully stop it. I just put a Band-Aid on the problem. If you love me and your family, you will go and fix yourself."

"This is not fair!" He shouted. "I am a victim, too! I opened up and told you about what happened to me when I was younger."

"Justin, you did, and I am so sorry that happened to you then. I'm sorry that you didn't get help when you were younger. But I can't afford to *not* help Sierra. I have to protect her. I just *have* to! You're an adult now. You need to take responsibilities for your own actions. I can't do this anymore. I feel so relieved that my sisters know. I felt like a prisoner in my own mind keeping your secret. You have to go."

"Where will I go?" he asked.

"Justin, you can go to your parents' house! Hell, they live down the street!" At that moment, I thought to myself, *Wow. It's a good thing his kids' mother moved out of his parents' house three months ago, or that would have been a real Jerry Springer situation!*

"I am *not* going to move back to my parents' house!" He shouted. "I'm a grown ass man!" The reality was that at that time, I really wasn't concerned about where he went. He just needed to leave our home. Period.

Justin gathered the rest of his stuff, packed it in his car, and was getting ready to leave. I asked for his house key. He reluctantly handed it over to me.

"Bree, you're making a big mistake, but have it your way," he said.

I honestly believe that Justin thought I was making a power move that would last for a few days, or maybe even a week, tops. That was on December 21st. I will always remember that day. It was a day after my bestie's birthday, and it would be the last time that Justin and I would ever share a home together.

My life was now in transition. I was uncertain of my next move, but I was confident that I'd made the right move. Nonetheless, I cried by myself for the next two hours.

I called Michelle and told her what had happened.

"Well, I'm glad you said something first," she said. Apparently, Sierra had opened up to Michelle and given her an earful of the truth. She was astonished at what she'd heard.

Michelle asked if I wanted to have the girls spend another night with her to give me some thinking room. I thanked her for offering, but I declined. I told her that I needed my girls at home with me more than ever. I needed to talk with them both to inform them of the change. Michelle understood, and she told me that if I needed anything, and she meant *anything*, not to hesitate to call.

I love my sister-girlfriends! That type of unconditional love is what carried me through my dark times... and more dark times were definitely ahead.

When Sierra and Kennedy finally made it home, my baby girl Kennedy was fast asleep. I tucked her cute little self in the bed with me. Sierra came into the room.

"Where is your husband?" she asked.

I told her that I wanted to talk to her. I started the conversation by opening up Justin's empty dresser drawers and showing her his side of the closet, which was now empty.

Her eyes opened wide. "*Really*, Mom?" she asked.

"Yes, Baby. Enough is enough. I'm not saying that I'm divorcing him, but he really needs to fix his issues, and he can't do it here anymore."

Sierra nodded her head in agreement and began to cry at the same time. "You chose *me* this time!" she cried. "Thank you, Mommy. I felt horrible all this time."

My daughter's words shook me. She'd believed that I had chosen Justin instead of her. In my mind, I thought that I was doing the right thing for the family and the marriage by keeping us together no matter what. Instead, I was sending the message to my beautiful baby girl that Justin mattered more than she did.

I embraced Sierra in a huge bear hug. Both of us were in tears. I was drained. Tomorrow, I had to tackle breaking the news to Kennedy, who was a big-time daddy's girl. I let out a big sigh and laid down. I went to sleep as soon as my head hit the pillow. I was knocked out.

Early the next morning, I was awakened by my phone ringing. My husband's name was on the caller ID.

"Hello?"

"Hey, what's going on?" I responded.

"Have you told the girls yet?" he asked.

"I told Sierra last night, but not Kennedy."

"I bet she was happy to hear that," he said.

"Justin, I don't think 'happy' is the right word. She was relieved that I believed her."

"So, you told her we are over?" he asked.

"No. I told her that you need to get help if you still want to be part of your family," I explained.

"Bree, I'm homeless!" he cried out.

"No you're not, Justin. You can stay at your parents' house," I said.

"I stayed in my car."

"That was your choice," I replied. "You know that your parents will allow you to stay with them."

"Can I see you today?" he asked.

"No, Justin. I don't think we should right now." This was an old game he played. I knew that all he wanted to do was to spend some time with me in order to play on my weakness.

"I'll let you go, Bree. *Clearly* you don't want to talk to me!" he said.

Before I could respond, he hung the phone up in my ear.

Kennedy, who was now eight years old, woke up and came into my room.

"Where's Daddy?" she asked.

I patted the edge of my bed, inviting her to come and lay down with me. She jumped into the bed.

"Daddy is not here."

"Will he be back soon?" she asked. Kennedy and Justin usually made pancakes together in the morning.

"No, Baby. Daddy and Mommy are taking a break from each other. Daddy won't be in our home for a while."

"Why, Mommy?" The tears welled up in her eyes.

"Daddy has some things that he needs to fix before he can come back home. He will always be your daddy, and he loves you immensely, but this has to be for right now. You can see him whenever you like. That, I promise."

Kennedy wiped the tears from her face. “Okay, Mommy. I just have one question.”

“Yes?”

“Does it have to do with him looking at Sissy?” she asked.

“What do you mean?” I replied defensively.

“Sissy cries a lot at night, and I heard her tell her friend, ‘He keeps watching me,’” Kennedy explained.

“Daddy has issues. Hopefully, he can fix them so he can come back home again,” I said.

“What if he doesn't, Mommy?”

Rather than answer her final question aloud, I thought to myself, *Then he can't come home. Period. The ball is in his court.*

I picked up the phone to call Mia and Scharae. Of course, they were both eager to know what had happened between Justin and me.

“Did you do it? No? Hello? Just get straight to the point!” Scharae ordered.

“Yes,” I simply said.

“Sister, did you get his key?” This time, the question came from Mia.

“Yep.”

“How was it?” Mia asked.

“It was hard. Emotional. I have to say, he didn't make a scene. He knew that we’re at the end of the road.”

“Girl, I can't believe you didn't tell us!” Scharae chimed in.

“I didn't know how or where to begin. So, I just didn't,” I confessed.

“How could you let this *happen*?” Mia asked. “As a mother, you're supposed to protect your kids, and you didn't.” The tone changed from supportive to argumentative.

"I completely understand why you guys are upset," I said. "I'm mad at me, too. I have no idea why I allowed it to go on for so long. I didn't know how to fix it. I tried to pray it away, ignore it away, and finally, hide it away."

Both Scharae and Mia detected that I was on a very sensitive emotional rollercoaster. They empathized with my feelings and decided to drop the subject for the moment.

"Well, he's out of the house now, so we're going in the right direction," said Scharae.

Christmas and New Years were a complete blur to me; I simply went through all of the necessary motions on autopilot for the sake of my girls. Although I wore the mask of being strong and confident in front of my daughters each day, each night when I took it off, I was totally depressed. Wine became my method of coping – anything to numb the pain.

Justin had informed me that he'd enrolled himself in a program that dealt with his type of issue. I thought to myself, *Okay. He's moving in the right direction now. Maybe there's a possibility that we can restore our marriage and family.* I tried to maintain a level of hope in the midst of what seemed like a hopeless situation.

Fortunately, I was excelling in my career during this time. Things were going really well at work, so well, in fact, that I got a big promotion and started making a lot more money. The position also offered me a lot more flexibility in my work schedule. I started to recognize how consistently I was receiving God's favor during this period of my life. I was spiritually focused again. The girls and I had begun faithfully attending church again, I'd started to really crave the Word of God and to receive His direction for my life.

I finally got up the courage to have a meeting with our pastor, the one who had married us. I informed him about what had transpired between Justin and me. He offered a prayer and empathized with our situation. He, as well as everyone else who knew about my situation, agreed that I was doing the right thing by asking Justin to leave. Protecting Sierra and Kennedy was to be my first priority. I was comforted that I was finally starting to wake up.

Despite the spiritual progress that I was making, I couldn't help but reflect back on what I had been doing over the past several years. The more time I spent apart from Justin, the more angry I became at him and at myself. I felt like an unfit mother for having allowed this craziness to continue for so long. I always wrestled with the word "allow." In my mind, I did not allow, condone or give the okay for Justin's actions! However, in fairness, I also did not stop them or separate me and my daughters from them. I'd only tried to make it more difficult for Justin to do these things. For me to have stopped his actions back then would have meant what I had just done: removing the problem from my household.

Justin eventually moved back into his parents' house, right down the street from me and the girls. Even though Justin was at their house and no longer in ours, I still felt suffocated because we were all living on the same block. Living in such close proximity to us also made it possible for Justin to still able to see all my moves.

For the next couple of weeks after I made Justin leave our house, I prayed for specific directions from God. I begged God to order all of my steps; I was fearful of stepping out on my own and making the wrong decisions again. I needed a clear-cut sign from God of what to do. Two weeks later, I got the sign.

One night, I was on the phone with my friend. I had my bedroom window ajar in order to ventilate the room. It was pretty late at night, so I told my friend that I was going to go to bed.

Not even five minutes later, I heard a man yelling, "I'm sick of this crap! That freaking weirdo's looking into the windows again!"

My heart dropped. I jumped out of the bed and raced to my window. It was my next door neighbor who had been yelling. The next thing that I saw was Justin; he was in a crawling position and moving quickly across the yard. Then, he got up and burst into a full sprint in the direction of his parents' house.

The commotion was so loud that both Sierra and Kennedy woke up.

"He's back at it, huh, Mom? Thought you said he was getting help? Don't think his therapy is helping," Sierra said. Her tone was sarcastic as she shook her head and carried her little sister back to her room. She intentionally slammed her bedroom door behind her.

I was shocked; I knew I had seen him. I called him. There was no answer. I walked around our home to ensure that every door was locked and every window was shut. My nerves were rattled. I went back to bed.

About 15 minutes later, there was knocking at my front door. The knocks were very strong and authoritative; the sound of the banging startled me. I was scared to answer, so I looked through the peephole. I saw the silhouette of two people standing in my doorway and red and blue flashing lights in the background. It was the police. I opened the door, and there stood two police officers, one male and one female.

"Evening, Ma'am. We received a call of a Peeping Tom in the neighborhood." My heart dropped again.

"Okay?" I said, as if I were clueless.

"Well, apparently a neighbor said it was your husband. Is your husband home?" the male officer asked.

"No. He and I are separated," I said.

Sierra walked out of her room. "What's going on, Mom?" she asked.

I shooed her away. I didn't need her offering any additional information to the police.

"Nothing," I said. "Go back to sleep." She looked directly at the officers, shook her head, and returned to her bedroom, again slamming her door. I continued my conversation with the officers.

"So, as I was saying, he and I are separated. We've been so for about a month." Then, I asked the officers, "How are you so sure it was my husband?"

The female officer quickly answered, "Your neighbor sees him daily," as if I had asked a stupid question. She continued, "It was reported that he was looking through your window, and your neighbor has witnessed him looking through other people's windows, too."

I screwed my face up as if I was shocked and confused. "I haven't seen him all day," I lied.

The officers gave me their card and said that if I happened to hear or remember anything, to please contact them. Then, they left.

I had asked for my steps to be ordered by God, and with this sign, He had pointed me in the direction I should go. This was my first encounter with God giving me a clear sign and me actually recognizing the sign and following through on it.

The next day, I started to look for a new place to live, a safe haven for me and my girls. It was time to leave the block and journey to the next level of faith that God was taking me to. When God makes a way for you, He makes it intentionally, and He blocks all obstacles that can get in the way. In my housing search, I only went to check out two places for rent out of my list of 20. The first place I loved, but for whatever reason, I did not get it. I was heartbroken, but still, I trusted God's plans. The very next day, I saw the second apartment on my list, liked it and got it.

Everything was moving super-fast for me. I'd just received a promotion with a substantial raise, and now we were moving. The girls and I were scheduled to move within two weeks. Blessing after blessing was being afforded to me.

I had been unhappy for quite some time about living on Justin's old childhood street, and he knew this. Therefore, I jumped on the very first opportunity that I had to move away from the street. The girls and I needed distance to breathe and to adjust to our new lives without Justin. Up until now, I had still been optimistic about salvaging our marriage. However, the setback of his recent peeping incident had put us right back to square one.

The hardest part about the move was breaking the news to Justin. I waited until the week before the girls and I received our official move-in date before notifying him. I was both nervous and anxious about letting Justin know about our plans to move. When he heard, he was mad and sad. He asked me how we could possibly salvage our marriage and family if I moved without him. He believed that once I started to live my life without him, it would inevitably mean the end of our relationship. At the time I thought he was wrong; I thought he was being overly sensitive about the move. I insisted that the move would be best for us, and my girls and I were going to make the move without him. Little did I know that our move would result in Justin showing his true colors, and this would ultimately be the demise of our relationship.

When moving day came, I was both excited and scared about my new beginning. A series of questions danced through my mind. *Am I making the right decision? Am I being true to my marriage vows? Will Justin be okay? Will the girls and I be alright?* The Holy Spirit showed me that all of these questions and doubts were coming from the enemy and that they were directly rooted in fear. However, God did not give me the spirit of fear; instead, He gave me the spirit of love, power and a sound mind, so I had to make a choice to walk in these things. I had to walk in truth and light. The more that I spoke the truth about the secret that I had been hiding, the less power it had over Sierra and me. The more I began to move out of the darkness by trusting in the Lord, the more His light shined on us.

We spent all day moving. On our final trip back to our old house to gather the last few items, Justin was in the house packing the remainder of his belongings. He looked so sad when he saw me. I told him that this was my last trip back to the house; I was leaving. I could see him fighting back tears as he persisted in telling me that he believed I was making a mistake.

"It was bad enough that you asked me to leave the house. I did, Bree, with no hesitation or fight. But now you're moving away! We are *still* married. You're *still* my wife," he said in a demanding tone.

"You are correct," I quietly responded, "but you are still sick." With tears streaming down my cheek, I gave him a kiss on his forehead and then walked out the door.

As I packed a few final knick-knacks into the trunk of my car, everyone on the street could see Justin walking slowly away and back to his parents' house, his possessions in hand.

I jumped into my car and went to meet Sierra and Kennedy at our new apartment. They were there with my cousins and nephew, who had helped us with the move. In this stage of my life, I had the spirit of nesting; I needed to provide my girls with a cozy home to help them transition from our dysfunctional period into a more functional, stable life. For a week or so, I worked diligently before and after work to make our apartment look and feel like a home.

I have to say that I did a good job; within a week, the boxes were packed away, the pictures were hung on the wall, and the cupboards, cabinets and closets were completely filled and organized. I had not given Justin my new address just yet; all he knew about where we'd moved to was the city. I needed some space and to establish some normalcy first.

I ensured that Justin was able to stay connected to Kennedy. She was his daughter, after all. Justin was able to call and talk with her every day. He would also go pick her up every day after school and bring her to his parents' house. Then, after work, I would drive to Justin's parents' house to pick Kennedy up and take her home. This not only gave Justin ample time to see his daughter, but it also gave him and me a chance to touch base and talk about his therapy sessions.

Over the course of our discussions, I became very curious about his issue, so I started to conduct my own research. The medical definition of a voyeur is 'a person who gains sexual pleasure from watching others when they are naked or engaging in sexual activity.' There were a lot of resources for the offenders and also for family members who were victims. I read a lot of online testimonies and stories about the successful outcomes of rehabilitation; however, I also read stories about people who had experienced outcomes that were quite the opposite.

Even with all of the information that I'd read and all of the resources that were available to me, I still felt alone and ashamed. I never went to a meeting. I believed that this was Justin's cross to bear. I had tried to help him in the past, but I'd only ended up making a bigger problem for all of us.

Now that Justin was no longer living with us, I was able to refocus my attention on Sierra. This was especially important because now, I was her only active parent. You see, on another occasion, Nigel and Justin had seen one another in the city, and they'd had an altercation. Allegedly, Nigel had flashed a concealed weapon to Justin and also called the cops on him. The next day, Justin went to the courthouse to file a complaint against Nigel, and since the judge believed Justin rather than Nigel, he granted Justin a three-year restraining order protecting the entire family from Nigel, Sierra included. This resulted in a falling out between Nigel and me and also prevented Nigel from being involved or in contact with Sierra. Because of this, unfortunately, Nigel did not get to celebrate some major milestones in Sierra's young life. Sierra was approaching her 16th birthday when the restraining order was first obtained, so Nigel had missed out on her 16th birthday party, homecoming, prom and graduation.

Now, Sierra was attending a local junior college. Although she had good grades, she yearned for more. A church friend contacted Sierra and invited her to a College Expo. Sierra thought it would be interesting, so she decided to check it out. When she returned home from the Expo, she talked to me about a university in the South in which she had taken interest. Out of all of the college booths that she'd visited at the Expo, she'd only picked up one application: it was for this particular college. I asked if she was serious about attending, and she insisted that she was. Sierra started the process and applied.

During this time, Justin was constantly asking for us to get back together. Each time he asked, I was very clear with him, saying, "Justin, let me focus on Sierra first. When she's all squared away, I can circle back to our relationship. Be as patient as she was when I put you first for all those years in the past. Continue on with your therapy, and get yourself together."

However, Justin couldn't do that… or he *wouldn't* do that. He wasn't patient at all. Instead, he was constantly trying to force me to put his feelings before Sierra's, a behavior which I grew to resent. This was a time in my life that I had dedicated to trying to help Sierra, not focus on him. Period! Fortunately, my support and focus on Sierra paid off. Exactly one month after she'd sent in her college application, we received the amazing news that she had been accepted to the college of her choice!

Justin didn't realize it, but at the time, I was testing his ability to not be so impulsive. After all, it was his impulses and his urges that had fueled his sickness for so many years. However, what *I* did not realize at the time was that while I thought that Justin was getting himself better, he still had a number of 'distractions' in his life.

Around the same time that Sierra received her college acceptance letter, I received a letter of my own; it was a surprising two-page letter that had been sent to my work e-mail address from "Miss 100."

In this email, Miss 100 went on a long, lengthy rant about a whole bunch of nothing, but she said that she had been able to deduce that I had a good man. She went on to explain that she and Justin had been on a date. *What the heck?* I thought. *First, some random girl contacts me with this mess on my work e-mail, then, she feels comfortable enough to reach out to me about my husband? Yes we're estranged, but none the less, he is still my husband!* I thought. After reading the letter, I was livid!

I reached out to my girls, Scharae and Mia, and I read the e-mail to them, word for word. However, at that moment, I realized something: I had been asking God for clarity and for which steps to take – in that order. In that moment, He gave me exactly what I'd been asking for, and I knew what I needed to do: I was going to move forward with a divorce.

The ironic part was that I'd had every intention of beginning the process of trying to restore my marriage after Sierra had gone off to college. I'd just never shared this with Justin. However, God had revealed to me what I needed to know within the timeframe that I needed to know it so that I wouldn't make such a huge mistake. This would not be the first time that God revealed things to me. It was actually just the beginning.

I printed a copy of the letter from my e-mail and went to pick up Kennedy from Justin's parents' house. When we were leaving, I politely slipped him the neatly-folded letter. I took the liberty to title it "Another Reason," and I made sure to hand it to Justin when Kennedy and I were pulling out. He smiled, thinking that it was a thoughtful love letter. I grinned at him as if to say, *No, it's not that at all!*

Before we even reached the freeway, Justin called my mobile phone, and he continued calling every few minutes. I ignored his calls all the way home. I wanted him to sit with and really feel the discomfort that the disturbing letter produced, just as I'd had to do when it had come to my work email earlier that day. Justin wasn't the only one I ignored; I never responded to Miss 100 either. I didn't feel like I needed to; she was irrelevant. I blocked her e-mail address so she could not reach out to me again.

I believe that because of my faith and the intimate walk with the Lord that I now had, I was able to see all of the things that God was revealing to me. I had asked God to reveal to me what I should do and to order my steps, and He had done just that. Was I hurt, bothered and annoyed? Absolutely. But on the other hand, since my separation from Justin, I had been less anxious and less stressed, and I was finally regaining some order for me and my girls. Heck, Sierra was preparing to go off to university, and my promotion at work was a huge blessing. Kennedy also seemed to be doing much better than I'd expected after Justin's and my separation, especially considering that she's a real daddy's girl. God was moving!

Most importantly, my walk with the Lord was becoming more intimate and consistent daily, not just for the favor that He had blessed my life with, but for His love and compassion. You see, when my girls were asleep, my sister friends were with their families, and I was crying, sad, depressed and lonely, God's love and comfort protected me. I knew that it was Him because I felt His presence. He eased my mind when the enemy tried to take it over.

When I got home from picking Kennedy up and delivering a copy of the letter from "Miss 100" to Justin, I was interested to find out just how long this indiscretion had been going on. Justin and I still shared the mobile phone bill, so I logged on to the internet and began to check the call history. I found out that the calls had begun prior to me asking him to move out and that he had been talking to her for a couple of months. I wasn't shocked; I was pissed off. Even with all that we were dealing with as a family, he was still untrue. In my mind, I was more sure than ever that there would be no more trying to salvage and restore our marriage. I refused to be obsessed with Justin and his antics any longer. I didn't have time for that.

Sierra, Michelle and I were due to fly south to Sierra's new university to settle her into her dorm. I was super grateful that Michelle had come with us. Michelle's heart is so big and loving, and she absolutely adored Sierra and did not want to miss celebrating this milestone with us. She also knew that I was going to be a big cry baby, and she could not see me going down there and saying goodbye without a support system. They say that it takes a village to raise a child, and I was certainly blessed with a great one.

The night before our trip, I laid in my bed trying to account for everything that had transpired in the past year. No one could have told me one year prior that this would be my life. Justin and I were separated, and I was on my way to start the process of a divorce. Nigel, Sierra and I still felt the strain between us. Sierra was getting ready to go to a university. I was blessed with a good promotion at my job. The girls and I had our own cozy apartment. Things sure had changed quickly.

My relationship with Sierra had gotten much better. I was glad that we still had each other, because at one point, this almost was not the case. You see, before we'd moved into our new apartment, Sierra had tried to commit suicide. She felt that my separation from Justin was all her fault; if she had not been around, she reasoned, I never would have had to make the decision to separate from him. One night, weeks before we moved from our old house to our new apartment, she'd taken a lot of pills. Fortunately, the Holy Spirit wouldn't let it be.

Sierra's body immediately rejected the pills, causing her to begin projectile vomiting. I woke up in the middle of the night after hearing her gag violently. Running to the bathroom where she was, I saw the empty pill bottles next to her. She and I spent the whole night on the bathroom floor, crying and praying.

There on the bathroom floor, Sierra shared with me that she didn't feel worthy enough to live; she had dreams, but she did not know how to reach them. For her, it seemed easier to let go of life than to reach for her goals. Sierra explained that she wanted to do something important with her life. Something meaningful. She would go on to major in criminal justice, because she desires to work with the FBI to help abused children. Can you imagine going from such a horrible flashback in which I'd almost lost my daughter to looking across my bedroom and seeing my suitcase packed for the early flight to begin her new future at a university? *My baby is a college student!* I thought. God had spared Sierra's life, and He'd awakened me. He was still giving me new mercies daily. If He didn't do another thing for me, I wouldn't complain.

As I lay on my pillow, I said a prayer and closed my eyes. We had a big day in the morning. *"Sierra season" begins now!* I thought, as I drifted off to sleep.

I woke up early the next morning; I had to drop Kennedy off at her Auntie Scharae's before heading to the airport with Sierra. Kennedy was excited to spend the week with Scharae and play with her cousin, Christian, Scharae's daughter. The two girls always had fun together, but they were *notorious* arguers! Fortunately, Scharae always knew how to handle them and their many fallouts.

Before Kennedy and I left for Scharae's house that morning, Kennedy kissed her big sister goodbye; they were both emotional. I arrived at Scharae's house and dropped

Kennedy off. Before I left, Scharae said a brief prayer for us, asking God to give us traveling grace and to place a hedge of protection around us. I kissed both Kennedy and Miss Christian. Then, I headed back home to meet my nephew at my apartment, as he was going to take us to the airport.

We arrived at the airport two hours before our scheduled flight departure time. Michelle met us there; when I saw her at the airport, I became emotional.

"This is really happening," I said, fighting back tears.

"Yes."

"Isn't God amazing?" I asked.

"Yes, ma'am! Indeed, He is," she replied.

Michelle is a huge reflector; she likes to think back on things that have happened in the past and God's faithfulness through them all. There in the airport, she recalled Justin's and my wedding, the birth of her god daughter, Kennedy, Justin's struggles with peeping, his issues with cheating, and our present status of being separated and headed for divorce. Then, she said something very profound to me.

"You have to admit, Bree. There were a lot of good times you guys shared."

I nodded my head in agreement.

"I have to admit, we did share some good times. The trips, the parties, our get-togethers. So many memories," I agreed.

I shared with Michelle that although I still loved Justin, I was not in love with him anymore.

"There's been a lot of water under the bridge and too many negatives to move forward toward a reconciliation. I honestly believe that God has something else in store for me. I don't know what it is, but everything is pointing towards a new life. The next level! I hate to admit it, but ever since we separated, I can honestly say that my life is better. I am better and so are my kids."

Michelle listened intently as I rambled on. Sierra was in her own zone at the airport. She had her Beats by Dre headphones on, and she was bobbing her head to music and texting away on her phone. We boarded the plane, had an uneventful flight, and landed safely and on time. We were excited about the adventure that awaited!

Our stay in Daytona Beach was a pleasant one. We handled all of Sierra's business and helped her to transition to her dorm and get registered for her classes. Dorm shopping was the absolute best! Sierra got everything she needed to have a comfortable stay and a successful semester.

You should have seen Michelle and me on the campus. You couldn't tell us a thing! We were high-fiving, fist-bumping, and making Sierra take *tons* of pictures. I think we embarrassed her! But hell, who cares? I would never be able to get those moments back, so Michelle and I took full advantage of the situation.

It was coming up to my last day with Sierra. I woke up feeling super emotional and anxious. I went into prayer, asking God to give me the strength to leave and not make Sierra scared or nervous. I thank the Lord for friends like Michelle. She didn't have to come with us to Florida. She has a family herself, but she said she was not going to miss this celebration. She'd also sarcastically joked, "Plus, who's going to hold *you* up? You *know* you're going to lose it!" She was correct. All of my sisters either called or texted me with encouraging words – Mia, Scharae, Charlie and Roxy. They all thanked Michelle for being there for me.

On our way back to the dorm to drop off Sierra, the ride was quiet. I tried to be as upbeat as possible.

"Well, Baby, I am *so* proud of you!" I said enthusiastically.

"Thank you, Mommy," she replied.

"You remind me so much of your grandmother. Your strength and your wisdom amaze me. You're going to do amazing things with your life. I can *feel* it! *God* placed you at this college at this time in your life. Nothing is an accident. All things work together," I said, encouraging her.

"I know, Mommy."

"Whenever you need me, I will be here for you, but even better than me is God. Promise that you'll go to Him first, even before me?" I asked.

"I promise!" Sierra said, smiling.

"That's where all of our help comes from," I continued. "You're my firstborn. We have a special bond. I love you, and I will miss you. Call me whenever. You're also fortunate to have aunties that have poured into your life. You can call them anytime as well."

Sierra turned the tables on me. I was here trying to make sure that *she* was going to be okay, but she was concerned about *me* being okay.

"Mom, are you going to be okay by yourself with Justin?" Sierra asked, concerned.

"You are the child, and I'm the mother. I'm going to be fine! Don't you fret over me. You hear me?" I asked.

"Yes, Ma'am," she answered.

When we arrived at her dorm to say goodbye, I hugged Sierra tightly. For a long time, I didn't want to let her go. I was trying to wipe away all my tears before she and I stopped embracing, but I couldn't. Sierra was crying, saying how much she was going to miss me and Kennedy. Then, she embraced her Aunt Michelle, who whispered something in her ear. They both laughed. As usual, Auntie Michelle slipped Sierra her a nice amount of money. I shook my head.

"You always spoil her!" I said.

Michelle laughed. "She is mine to spoil!"

I said goodbye to my baby again and somehow managed to walk out the dorm room. Michelle and I headed to the airport.

I kept chanting in my mind, *My baby is in college! My baby is in college!* I had a shout in my spirit and praise on the inside. I thanked Michelle for just being her and loving on me and the girls effortlessly. As we boarded the plane on our way home, I thought to myself, *Well, now it's just me and my Kennedy. Just the two of us now.*

A few months passed, and I was in contact with Sierra daily. She was adjusting well to college life, and I was adjusting to having only one kid to parent. Kennedy and I started to find our groove with our morning drop-offs and after school pick-ups. My work life was steady and successful, and I was trying to feel less overwhelmed by the day. However, my heart was always heavy from thinking about how I'd left things with Nigel. I wanted him to know that Sierra was in college and thriving. Scharae was able to give him updates and highlights about Sierra, as she and Nigel attended the same church. Although I was grateful for Scharae being able to keep Nigel in the loop, I also felt guilty that these updates were not coming from me or Sierra. Despite this glitch, however, I felt that God was restoring me and my life during this season.

One particular afternoon, I headed out to lunch. I usually go to lunch at the same time every day, but for some reason, on this day, I went about three hours late. On my way out of the office building, I called Mia to see how her day was going.

"Why the super late lunch?" she asked. I chuckled and explained that I had been in the zone at work and needed to finish the project that I had been working on before going to lunch.

As I walked down the street on my way to the café, I heard someone call my name.

"Bree!"

I looked up, and right in front of me was Nigel in his truck. When our eyes connected, we both smiled. Because I knew Nigel, I also knew that his smile was an indication that he was open to a conversation. I quickly motioned for him to pull over. He did.

"Oh, my God!" I anxiously scream-whispered to Mia on the phone.

"Who is that?" Mia asked curiously.

"Girl, it's Nigel! He is pulling over now!"

"Wow! How crazy! You were just talking about wanting to reach out to him the other day. Now, here's your chance!"

"I know! Pray for me, Sister," I said.

"Call me later with the details, okay?"

"I will," I said. I hung up the phone.

Nigel parked his truck and waved me over. I nervously walked over to him.

"How are you?" I asked in a friendly voice.

"I'm good, and you?" Nigel answered.

"A lot has transpired in three years," I said.

"I know," he replied. His voice was a bit stern.

"First of all, I owe you an apology," I began. I explained to him how sorry I was about all that had happened. Nigel listened intently. Then, I announced, "Justin and I are separated and in the process of getting a divorce."

"I know. I heard," he responded. "There was a lot of emotion and confusion happening with us all at once. It was hard for me to decipher what was true or false. You hurt me, Bree, by not allowing me to be able to parent our daughter. I've missed out on so much of her life that you didn't."

"And for that," I said, "I am genuinely and sincerely sorry. You hurt me with the lies that she was being touched. The truth was already enough. Why did you have to embellish?"

"What? Embellish? What are you talking about? I was informed by the lady from Child Protective Services that there were allegations of physical and sexual abuse!" he said.

"That's a lie! He never touched her. Nigel, that is why I was so mad at you!" I said. I told him I had an official letter from CPS stating that the investigation showed no proof of sexual assault.

"Again, Bree, I never said that," Nigel said.

My typically one-hour lunch turned into two hours. Nigel and I talked through all of the misconceptions and misunderstandings between us. I cried, we laughed, and we caught up on what had been happening in both of our lives. Then, Nigel gave me the biggest gift that I could ask for: forgiveness.

Nigel said that he had forgiven both Sierra and me for our part in the drama. I forgave him as well. He expressed that he was eager to talk with Sierra so that they could start the healing process with one another. I agreed that this process needed to happen, and I encouraged him to reach out to her soon.

Before parting, Nigel and I made sure that we had each other's updated contact information. Then, we hugged and left. I believe that we both walked away feeling relieved, hopeful for continued healing, and optimistic about the potential of slowly regaining trust for one another with time. I knew that our meeting was neither luck nor a coincidence. It was favor from the Lord!

I could not wait to call Sierra and give her the good news! I could sense that she had been missing her father, but I had not known how to address her feelings, because I knew that I had played a key role in creating the distance that existed in their relationship. I called Sierra a few times but kept getting her voicemail. *She must be in class,* I thought.

Sierra finally answered my call.

"Hey, Mom. What's up? Is everything good? I see that you called a few times. I was in class."

"I figured that, Baby. Sorry for calling so much. I just had some really good news, and I couldn't wait to share it!"

"Did you divorce Justin?" she joked sarcastically.

"Very funny! No. But guess who I ran into today on my lunch break?"

"Mom, sorry. I'm so bogged down with studying, my brain is on overload. Can you just tell me, please?" she asked.

That's no fun, I thought to myself.

"Your dad!" I exclaimed.

There was silence on the other end of the line for about 10 seconds. For a moment, I thought I had lost the connection.

"Hello? Hello?"

Sierra came back. "My dad? What happened?"

"*God* happened, Baby Girl!" I excitedly shouted. "We had a great talk. I cried, laughed, and we even argued a bit. But nonetheless, we both agreed that you are most important and our main priority. He would like for you to call him."

The news was a bit overwhelming, and Sierra broke out crying. "Mommy, what do I say?"

"The truth, Baby. However you feel. He's still your dad, and he loves you. We were all wrong to some degree, but God is giving us an opportunity to restore what's been broken. We need to be obedient and humble ourselves to the process," I explained.

"Okay, Mommy," she said.

I gave her Nigel's number and told her to pray before calling him.

After Sierra called her father, she called me back to let me know that they'd had a beautiful conversation that was apologetic, raw and compassionate. I was grateful. Sierra now had her father back in her life, and they were rebuilding their relationship and taking things one step at a time. *Isn't God something amazing?* I thought. The consistent favor and grace that He had showered upon me and my girls was astonishing! I knew that I was not worthy; yet, God had continued to order my steps and provide for us.

Justin and I were still separated and in the process of executing the paperwork for our divorce. I was in constant prayer for clarity that a divorce was the right step for me. It seemed like every time I had the inkling to try and work things out between us, something always happened to point me in the direction of divorce. *Every* single time, like clockwork! Either I heard rumors of him and other women, or he got so frustrated and impatient with me that he would cuss me out, saying hurtful things about me or my mother. The blatant disrespect was vicious.

After developing an intimate relationship with God and realizing just how much He cared for me, I could not and would not subject my girls or myself to that type of energy anymore. I realized now that a divorce would be my reality, so I began to separate myself from the past. I no longer frequented the same places to which he and I used to go together, and I stopped hanging around our old friends. This was extremely difficult for me, because I loved our friends. However, my detachment from them was very necessary for my sanity and growth.

Unfortunately, this also meant that I had to leave our church, the one in which Justin and I had been married. I was heartbroken; the girls and I were very fond of our church and our church family. This decision was also extremely difficult, but again, it was a very necessary one.

The ironic part about me leaving my church was that we ended up at Scharae and Nigel's church. I was very familiar with this church because in the past, when Mia would come into town, the three of us would always attend the service together. I'd always loved the vibe, the youth, the youthfulness of the church, and the pastor's teaching. After my separation from Justin, I had wanted to begin attending this church with my bestie, Scharae. However, after Nigel and I fell out over the custody drama with Sierra, I purposely chose not to attend the church. I knew that I would see him there, and I wanted to avoid him.

Thankfully, things were different now that Nigel and I were cool with one another again. The Saturday night before I was to visit the church, I called him to give him the heads up that I was coming to visit his church. I'd just wanted to touch base with him before seeing him again. Nigel was very gracious. He extended an invitation for me to visit the church, said I should definitely come, and told me that the services were great and that his bishop was anointed.

Attending this new church was an easy transition for Kennedy; she was already very familiar with it, having visited a number of times in the past. Whenever I went out of town for business, Kennedy would stay at Scharae's house, and of course, she went to church with Scharae's daughter, Christian. Kennedy absolutely loved the children's program at the church, and when I told her that we were going to begin regularly attending the church, she was super excited.

The moment that Kennedy and I began attending the church, I could feel God's hands on me heavily. I frequently attended Sunday services, and this transitioned into me also attending the church's mid-week Bible study. Eventually, I also started to serve in volunteer ministry at the church. I felt very connected to the congregation.

During this time, I was also trying to co-parent Kennedy with Justin. To say that doing so was a challenge would be an understatement! I still loved Justin, but I was no longer in love with him. Nonetheless, he always did his best to try to get back together with me; although we were separated, he never missed a birthday, Mother's Day or Valentine's Day without giving me some gift, flowers or token of his love. However, I'd also heard that he didn't miss anyone else's either.

In our dealings with one another, we began to go through a horrible cycle by constantly arguing, then realizing that it was not just about the two of us; it was about Kennedy. Then, we would try to regain some form of normalcy to co-parent again. The cycle continued; we operated according to the same pattern over and over again. "Dysfunctional," I think, is the correct term for that behavior.

Although I talk about Justin's shortcomings, by no means is it my intent to paint him as a demon and me as an angel. I wasn't completely innocent myself. During our separation, I started to try and see other guys; however it never worked. After several failed attempts at dating, and because I was still legally married and did not want to be labeled a hypocrite, I'd stopped dating. It was hard, because I felt lonely and desired companionship, but it was also necessary; it was unwise to date in this season of my life.

I was fortunate to have some great sister friends who gave me wise, spiritual advice. Mia, Scharae, and Charlie were always on me the most when it came to me dating while I was separated but still married. At the time, all three of them would get on my nerves with their opinions and unsolicited advice about my dating life. However, thinking back, during that season of my life, I was blessed to have access to such wise counsel. They held me accountable to doing what was right and doing things the right way, and accountability is the key.

I had no excuse for making such unwise decisions. I had been getting the Word at church, and I knew right from wrong. The last thing that I wanted was for the enemy to laugh at me as I was falling into the deliberate temptations that he set before me because my flesh was weak and lonely. Being in limbo was not working for me; I surely wasn't going back to Justin, but I also couldn't move forward with my life because I was still tied to him, both legally and spiritually. Understanding that I couldn't have my cake and eat it, too, I decided that I needed to move the divorce process along.

As I became more comfortable with fellowshipping with some of the other church members, I was fortunate to connect with some amazing people and build some beautiful relationships. I grew very close to one particular group of ladies at the church. Within a short time span, we really meshed. Guess who was a part of this group? Tiny, the courthouse clerk! How ironic is that?

I had completely forgotten that when I'd seen her at Scharae's 40th birthday party, Tiny had told me that she and Scharae went to church together, so when I saw her at the church, I was shocked to see her there. I had no clue that she and Scharae had such a tight sister bond. I mean, I'd heard Scharae reference a girlfriend in the past whom she simply referred to as "T," but I had no idea that she was talking about the woman from the courthouse, Tiny.

By His divine hand, God strategically positions people to be a part of our lives. You see, my first introduction to Tiny was at the courthouse in the midst of my storm. At that time, I was very defensive and critical, and I did not want to like her. To me, she was just a friend of Nigel, the man who had become my new enemy. All I saw that day was her and Nigel chatting about what I'd assumed was our court case. However, what the enemy means for destruction, God will use for His glory. God had another plan that I could not see at the time.

Tiny was also in the middle of a divorce herself. Like me, she had been through the ringer of trying to juggle co-parenting and past hurts, and finding a balance between the two had been a challenging process. This shared experience was our common denominator. After we connected, we took our time learning about one another. She prayed for me, counseled me and loved me. In time, not only had we developed a relationship through the collective sisterhood of the other ladies in the group, but we also built our own individual relationship with each other, one-on-one.

In the beginning, Tiny and I had only become open to giving one another a chance because of our shared connection through Scharae. Scharae and Tiny were very close. To this day, if you ask them how they initially came to be friends, they will laugh and say, "We honestly don't know! It just happened!" However, nothing "just happens." God is always working and He is always perfect in what He does.

Today, ironically, I love Tiny like a sister. Our relationship was always in God's plan! Sierra and Kennedy now have another auntie who loves them dearly. I would often overhear Kennedy and Christian having conversations about which auntie they believed was the strictest between their Auntie Mia and their Auntie Tiny. They both agreed, hands down, that the trophy would go to Auntie Mia!

My season of seeking was one in which God hid me in the valley as He prepared my heart and my mind for greater intimacy with Him. This allowed Him to take me to a new level, both in my natural and spiritual life. Things started to fall into place.

Because Tiny and I shared such a close a friendship, I was able to ask her pertinent questions about my divorce process. The forms and legal verbiage were completely unfamiliar and overwhelming to me. I took a couple of days off of work to make time to go down to the courthouse and fill out a fee waiver for my divorce decree. In my mind, I thought, *Why should I have to pay for a divorce? I didn't commit a violation against Justin. He violated me!*

On three different occasions, I petitioned the court for a fee waiver, and every time, the judge denied my request, stating that I made too much money. I thought, *Wait. What? I'm a single mother of two, with one minor and one child attending an out-of-state university. Are you kidding me?* I felt so defeated.

I started to feel depressed. *Why, God?* I asked. I knew that if I didn't start the process myself, Justin never would. When I brought up with Justin the financial challenges that I was facing in trying to file for the divorce, he could not have cared any less. He made it crystal clear to me that he did not want the divorce anyway, so paying for it would be my responsibility. He said that if I really wanted it, I would make it happen. Everything was on me.

I *did* really want the divorce, but I had already assumed so much financial responsibility that I was maxed out. The fact that I was having a hard time getting the funds to file for divorce together did not bother Justin at all. In fact, he'd cold-heartedly explained to me that he didn't need a divorce decree to start another relationship with a new woman; a piece of paper wasn't going stop him from dating other people. I believed this, coming from Justin; I knew the caliber of women that he associated with, and it wouldn't matter to them one way or the other whether he was officially divorced or not. I, on the other hand, wanted to try to do things the opposite way. The right way.

I fondly remember this next incident like it was yesterday. One morning, as I was getting ready for work, I was looking in the mirror and applying my makeup. Nothing out of the ordinary. All of a sudden, I heard a voice say, "You will get the divorce, and you will not have to do a thing."

I can still remember the sensation that I felt from the calm vibration of the warm, authoritative voice. It was the same voice that had encouraged me to tell Mia and Scharae the truth in the hotel room after Scharae's birthday party. It was the Holy Spirit. When I heard His voice, I was neither afraid nor alarmed. Instead, I was comforted. I believed the words that He had just spoken to me, and I felt assured in that very moment. I wasn't sure how everything was going to play out, but what I did know was that it would all be taken care of. This divorce was not my battle; it was the Lord's. I immediately went into worship, praising God for His abundant grace and new mercies, completely in awe of His provisions and mightiness!

Now that I was in the process of actively cultivating an intimate relationship with God, I could hear the voice of the Holy Spirit clearly. However, on this particular morning, I remember wondering, *How many times did I hear God's voice in the past without being able to recognize it? How much did I miss out on when I lacked the ability to understand that God was talking to me?*

I pose these questions to you, as well. Are you in an intimate relationship with God so that you can hear His voice clearly, or is He trying to say things to you that you cannot hear because you can't recognize His voice? What might you possibly be missing out on because you lack the ability to hear the voice of the Holy Spirit?

If you cannot hear the voice of God, it is NEVER too late to begin a close, intimate relationship with Him and allow Him to speak to you. He talks to all of those who are in proper relationship with Him daily; we just need to learn how to drown out the constant noise in our lives and focus in on Him and what He's saying.

I never uttered a word to my girls about my second encounter in which I'd heard God's voice so clearly. I'd learned that everything that God talks to you about or instructs you to do is not meant for everyone to hear. It should be kept sacred, because it was given just to you.

After that encounter, every moment that I felt discouragement about not being able to file for divorce yet, I reflected back on the words that God had spoken to me. I did not know when I was going to be released from the marriage. I just knew that I would only have to do the bare minimum, and then the marriage would be dissolved. In my waiting for the manifestation of the promise that God had spoken to me, because I did not know the *exact* date and time it would come to pass, my faith and patience would be tested. I had no idea just how much.

Eventually, because we were co-parenting, I had to give Justin my new home address; I felt that he deserved to know the exact address where his daughter lived in case of an emergency. I also felt that he deserved to know my new address since we were still legally married. Justin was tasked with picking Kennedy up from school, helping her with her homework, and making her dinner. This was their bonding time, and it was his way of staying connected to his baby girl, whom he loved dearly.

Justin moved out of his parents' house to a city nearer to my apartment. Now that he had a steady job again, he seemed to be doing well for himself. He was able to begin financially assisting with Kennedy's daily needs, which relieved me a bit. For that, I was thankful.

Our daily encounters varied, depending a lot on how the wind blew that day. One day we were cool, and the next, we would be bickering. The uncertainty of what might happen as I went into each of our encounters made me very anxious.

In Justin's mind, we were still married, so we should at least be having sex with each other. In my mind, I was both single and hurt, and the thought of being intimate with him felt wrong and confusing. Plus, I was sure that he did not desire me specifically; he was a man who just had a huge sexual appetite.

What Justin really wanted was guilt-free sex. He would always say, "We're still married, so it's legal." *How romantic,* I would sarcastically think to myself. Then, I would simply respond, "Ummm, no thank you!"

Rejection was Justin's biggest pet peeve, so much so that he would literally get enraged when I would say "No" to him about anything or ignore his calls. If, after I chose not to answer his call for a period, I finally did answer, I would have to deal with his bad attitude. To show that he was pissed off at me for not acknowledging his call initially, he would retaliate, proceeding to call me 15 to 25 times, back-to-back. I would be so annoyed and embarrassed. It didn't matter who I was with or what I was doing; he would call relentlessly, so much so that anyone who was with me at the time would get annoyed as well. It became obsessive. Justin's behavior should have been a red flag for me; however, I brushed it off as being more of an annoying habit of his than being a sign from God.

The next red flag happened when Justin moved from his new place, which was a couple of cities away from me, to MY CITY! He actually moved into my neighborhood, a block-and-a-half away from me. I was floored. He told me that his move was not intentional; it was just where he'd found the best available apartment for the best price, and it was in an area that he liked. My gut feeling told me different.

Now, Justin and I shopped at the same grocery stores, filled up our cars at the same gas station, and went to the same local eateries. It felt like he appeared everywhere I went; I started to see him randomly all over the place. The only person who was happy and benefitted from Justin being so close to us was Kennedy.

This was the beginning of Justin stalking me. My once safe and cozy apartment started to not feel so safe and cozy anymore. Justin would drive into my parking area to see if I had any visitors, and then he would call or text me and describe to me, in detail, the car that was parked in my space. Because he did not know whether the car belonged to a male or female guest who was visiting my house, he called me every hoe and slut under the sun.

One Saturday evening, Justin called to speak with Kennedy. I told him that Kennedy was not with me; she was spending the night over at Scharae's house, because she and Christian had wanted to have a sleepover. I told him that I would have Kennedy call him back tomorrow after church, when she would be back home with me. Right away, Justin was pissed off. He believed that any time I didn't have Kennedy with me, it was because I'd sent her away so that I could have sex with someone.

After I finally got sick of the back-and-forth of another dysfunctional argument with Justin, I hung the phone up on him. I had plans to go on a date that night with an old friend. I glanced at the clock and decided that it was time to start getting ready.

Before long, something told me to look out of my living room window. As I looked out, I saw Justin walking across my walkway, heading towards my stairwell. I was so startled, my heart felt as if it was going to leap outside of my body! *What the hell is he doing here?* I thought, fuming. I grabbed my phone to call him and to furiously inform him that he had been caught. I had seen him with my own eyes!

Before I could connect the call, I received a text from my date. It said, "I'm here. Just parking. Be up in a few."

This can't be happening! I thought. I was in a state of panic. My estranged husband, who was in stalker mode, and my date were both at my house!

"K." I replied to the text, as if everything was all good. Meanwhile, I was a *wreck*!

I quickly called Justin. He answered his phone calmly, the opposite of me.

"What the hell are you doing here?" I asked. Enraged, I was yelling at the top of my lungs.

"What are you talking about?" he responded, as if I had just hallucinated seeing his image at my door.

That was when I completely lost it. I didn't have the time to play around and go back and forth with him. I knew what I had seen, and I knew that my date was on his way up to my door.

"I just saw you at my steps!" I yelled.

Justin hung up his phone without replying.

Just then, there was a knock at my door. I didn't know *who* it was. Was it Justin, or was it my date? I quietly tiptoed to my door and sprang up on my toes to look through the peep hole. It was my date! I was relieved for a millisecond as I hurriedly let him in. I wasn't sure if Justin was nearby.

My date was immediately able to pick up that something was off. "Is everything good, Bree?" he asked with an awkward smile.

"Yeah, yeah... I'm good!" I said, trying to cover up my anxiety. "I was just trying to get things in order before you arrived, and I fell a bit off track. No biggie!" I forced out a fake laugh, trying to act as nonchalant as possible. Meanwhile, my heart was racing, pounding a mile a minute.

"Are you ready to go, Bree? I made reservations before our movie," he said.

After seeing Justin, I didn't want to leave my apartment *at all.*

"Uhhh, one sec," I said. "I just need to call and check on my little one before we leave. I have some wine in the fridge. Help yourself!"

"No worries," he replied. "Would you like a glass, too, before we head out?"

"Sure," I said as I walked towards my bedroom with my phone in hand.

I had grown so tired of being embarrassed by Justin's excessive phone calls that now, I usually kept my phone on vibrate mode when I was around other people. I closed my bedroom door and glanced at the phone screen: he'd already called 16 times. I thought to myself, *This is going to be a crazy night for sure!*

My gut feeling was to not leave the house, but how was I going to explain that to my date? Either it was going to sound weird, or he was going to get the wrong impression and think that I only wanted to have sex with him. If he did think this, who could fault him for having such a thought. After all, any guy who'd shown up to take a woman on a date, only for her to say, out of the blue, "Let's stay in tonight" without telling him the whole story about *why* she wanted to stay in might think the same thing.

In that instant, I remembered that I was *not* that woman anymore. *I don't HIDE anymore*! I reminded myself. I took a deep breath and walked back into the living room. I admitted to my date that he had been correct in reading me; everything was *not* alright. I explained to him that my ex had recently been displaying obsessive behaviors towards me, constantly calling me and making unannounced pop-ups at my house and other random places.

My date said that he could tell that I was bothered, and he agreed that it would be cool to stay in. He called the restaurant and cancelled his reservation, and then he ordered Thai food delivered to my apartment. We stayed up talking and laughing for the majority of the night. My phone continuously rang, nonstop.

Shortly after midnight, my date left. I thanked him for a good time and for his understanding. He was such a gentleman! He never once tried to take advantage of the vulnerable state that I was in as a result of the situation. He said goodnight and gave me a kiss.

I was exhausted. I went into my bedroom and looked out of the window at the parking area. I saw Justin sitting in his car, staring at my window. Then, I saw my date walking towards his own car. Justin started his engine and started to follow my date. I panicked.

I stepped away from the window, grabbed my phone, and quickly called my date.

"Hey. The guy in the blue car? That's my *ex*!" Although I tried to maintain a calm voice, he could hear the terror behind it.

"Okay," he said calmly.

"Is he following you?" I asked.

"He's behind me, driving. I'm walking to my car. Don't worry. It's all good. Dude should do what's best for him and not say anything to me. I'll call you when I get to my car. Okay?" Before I could respond, he disconnected the call.

I went back to the window to see if I could see Justin, but I was unable to.

A few minutes later, my date called me back.

"Hey, are you alright?" I asked as soon as I picked up the phone. "I was so *concerned*!"

He laughed. "Of course I'm alright. The main question is, are *you*?" I let out a sigh of relief.

"Yes, I am," I replied. "I'm *so* sorry. It was not my intention to bring unnecessary drama to your life. Did he say anything to you?"

"Nope, not a word. He followed me to my car, and when I jumped in, he drove off. Bree?" he asked, waiting for me to answer so he could have my full attention.

"Yes?"

"I'm concerned for you. Dude doesn't seem like he's wrapped tight. I noticed your phone going off a lot while I was there, so I figured something was up. So, that is why you didn't want to go out, huh? Not cool to live your life that way!"

"I know." I was so embarrassed.

"Call me if you need anything," he said.

"Okay, thanks."

"No prob," he said before he hung up the phone.

I went back to my bedroom window, and there was Justin again, sitting in his car and staring at my window. I was scared. For the remainder of the evening, which was now early morning, my phone kept vibrating. I dozed off a bit, and when I woke up later in the morning, I looked at my phone screen. I had 86 missed calls and 12 text messages. Baffled, I began to read the texts. Justin was clearly irate. He'd actually used emojis to threaten my safety.

I called Scharae in tears. I was scared. I told her what had transpired the night before. She asked if Justin was still there, and I told her that he was; it appeared that he'd been there the whole night. Just then, I heard loud knocking at my front door. It was Justin.

"It's Justin! He's pounding on the door!" I said to Scharae, panicking.

"Open the door, Bree!" I heard Justin yell loudly.

"He's telling me to let him in!" I cried.

"You *better not* open that damn door, Bree!" she yelled back at me.

I started to scream at Justin at the top of my voice, "Leave me alone! Go away! Go away!"

Justin kept knocking. His voice went from yelling to calmly saying, "Just open the door. I want to talk to you."

Before I knew it, Scharae had made a three-way call, connecting me with the local police department in my city. She gave them my address and quickly told them what was happening at my house. Everything was such a blur, but I could clearly hear the lady dispatcher say that units had been dispatched and were en route. I felt nauseated.

Scharae instructed me to calm down and get myself together so the officers could walk me to my car and I could meet her and the kids at church.

"That's where you need to be for *sure*! Justin has lost his rabbit ass mind!" she hollered.

I did as she said. I quickly jumped into the shower and threw some clothes on in record time to get ready to go to church. I got dressed so fast because I didn't want the cops to come without me being ready to leave. Meanwhile, Justin was still outside, sitting in his car.

Just as I'd hurriedly begun to apply a bit of makeup, I heard another knock at my door. At this point, my nerves were utterly shot!

"Who is it?" I nervously yelled out.

"The police," a man answered. His voice was so authoritative. I opened the door, and there stood two male police officers in front of me. I invited them in and began to tell them the story of what had happened the night before.

"Do you have a restraining order?" one of the officers asked.

"No, Sir, I do not," I answered.

"I recommend that you petition the court for a restraining order for your protection," he advised. I listened intently.

I asked if they had seen Justin outside, and they informed me that they had; another unit was currently speaking to him. They said that they were unable to arrest him, but they would warn him that his actions were classified as stalking and that he could be arrested if he continued with such behavior.

I asked the officers if they would not mind waiting for just a few minutes while I gathered my things so they could walk me to my car. They graciously waited.

As soon as I got on the freeway, I called Scharae.

"All is well. I'm on my way to church," I said.

"Good! See you soon, Sister."

I remember pulling up to the church and admiring what a beautiful, sunny day it was outside, despite the unfortunate way in which my morning had begun. I parked my car and walked inside the church.

When I found Scharae and the girls, I was so happy just to see Kennedy's little face! She was a sight for sore eyes. I hugged and kissed her as she grinned and hugged me back. I was glad that she had no idea what had happened between her father and me. I looked over at Scharae, she could instantly tell that I was fighting my tears from falling; she was doing the same thing.

"Are you okay, Sister? You're safe now," she said as she comforted me with a big hug. I nodded in agreement. My heart was filled with gratefulness.

Scharae and I checked our girls into children's church and headed to the sanctuary. Tiny had already saved us a seat; we always sat together during the worship services. During praise and worship, I was so overwhelmed and consumed with thankfulness to the Lord. Things could have taken a turn for the worse, both last night *and* this morning; the situation could have had a tragic, grave outcome. However, He wouldn't let it be! I kept saying to myself, *BUT GOD! Thank*

You for Your grace, mercy, and protection, God, I cried out to Him.

When our bishop started the process of bringing us the Word that morning, for some reason, he was unable to.

"When the Holy Spirit is present," he said, "you give the Holy Spirit the platform."

The bishop started to prophesy and invite people to come down to the altar if they were suffering from some sort of physical ailment that he described. People who were suffering from whatever the bishop saw or felt made their way to the altar, where he and the deacons laid their hands on them and prayed over them.

Then the bishop said, "Someone, this morning, has dealt with a very traumatic situation. It's domestic... something happening at home. You need prayer."

A few people went down to the altar. Scharae and I looked at each other.

"No! It *can't* be," I said. She nudged for me to go down, and I did.

The bishop laid hands on everyone at the altar, and when he got to me, he prayed and touched me on my forehead. Then, he moved on to the lady who was standing next to me and prayed for her.

What he did next blew my mind. He came *back* to me! He laid his hand flat on the middle of my stomach and pressed it, as if he had been instructed by God to do so.

"My GOD!" the bishop said, as if he could feel all of the hurt, the pain, the rejection, the secrets, the ugliness and insecurity, and every bad decision that I had been harboring for years.

There are no words that could accurately describe the sensation I felt when my bishop prayed for me. At once, all I remember was a warm sensation washing over my body. I wasn't scared; I could feel the Holy Spirit holding me.

Minutes later, I woke up on the floor, still at the altar. I had been covered with a cloak, and I was lying in Scharae's lap. I had been RELEASED! What I experienced at the altar that morning was life changing for me.

ten

Beauty for Ashes

Justin and I still continued the horrible cycle of arguing while trying to co-parent Kennedy. My calling the cops on him that memorable Sunday morning had driven him to such a place of anger and disgust that he'd actually started the process of divorce on his own! In my heart, I knew that God was moving on my behalf, staying true to His promise. Just as the Lord had spoken to me, I was not going to have to do any leg work for our divorce!

Unfortunately, Justin's stalking only escalated. Anywhere that I went, I was confident that I would see Justin. It seemed like everywhere I was, so was he. It got so bad that he started to drive to my job every morning. I saw him on a few occasions driving up and down the street where my church was, and also at Kennedy's school. If he saw me in the company of my girlfriends, he wouldn't say anything, but if I was by myself or with Kennedy, he would ask to talk to me. Sometimes I would talk to him, and other times I wouldn't. If

Kennedy was with me, I would talk to him because he was still her father, after all, and I did not want to alarm her by telling her that we couldn't stop and talk to him. If I was by myself, I would either say "No," or I would agree to have just a few brief words with him.

I started to save Justin's threatening text messages and also began to take and save screen shots of his excessive phone calls, just in case I ever needed to use them as evidence in order to get a restraining order against him. I honestly never wanted to put Kennedy's father in jail. I just needed him to stop his antics. However, it seemed that he could not control his urge to terrorize me.

Mia gave Justin the nickname "Isis." Whenever I was talking to her and Scharae on the phone and we were discussing Justin, we used this code name for him so that Kennedy and Christian would not know who we were referring to in our conversations.

Even with all of Justin's foul behavior, God still tried to give him a way out; the Lord was trying to orchestrate the events of Justin's life so that he would stop his antics and realize that he was doing exactly what the enemy wanted him to do. This was an enemy who was playing for keeps, one that was trying to destroy his life.

In a matter of two short months, Justin's new car was totaled. Thankfully, he was not in the car at the time of the accident. However, because he did not have transportation, it was now a strain for him to get to and from work. This made it difficult for him to earn the money that he needed in order to pay his rent. Thus, Justin ended up having to move.

As a result of the move and lack of transportation, Justin neither lived blocks away from me anymore, nor did he have the ability to randomly pop up at my apartment or in my neighborhood.

I genuinely felt bad that he'd had to deal with two such major setbacks, back-to-back. However, during one of my intimate worship times with the Lord, God showed me that these events were necessary, that Justin having a car and living such a short distance away from my apartment were dangerous. I believed that God had allowed these things to be removed from Justin's life because the enemy was going to try to use them as tools to destroy him. By removing his car and taking his nearby residence, God was saving Justin from himself.

Talking to Justin afterwards, I did my best to try to appeal to his ability to see that maybe this was all a blessing in disguise.

I said, "You were spinning out of control. I don't think that you're out to hurt me, but I do believe that it could have happened, because you were being fueled by emotion and rage. That concerned me."

Justin thought that I was being cold and heartless and that I was secretly finding joy in his situation. That was the furthest thing from the truth. I never wanted Justin to suffer.

A few weeks after my encounter at the altar, I was in my car, headed to work. As usual, I was on our morning conference call. However, today, it was just me and Scharae on the line, because Mia had been unavailable to join the conference call that morning.

As I drove along the freeway talking to Scharae, I heard the voice of the Holy Spirit as clear as day. It was the third time I'd heard His voice this clearly in my life. He said, "You have to tell your story."

"What?" I asked out loud. This confused Scharae; she had not been talking at the time. Then I politely said, "No, thank you," as if I was politely declining a beverage that I had been offered.

"Girl, what you talking about? No, thank you? I didn't offer you anything," Scharae said, puzzled.

Tears started to flow from my eyes. I knew exactly what He meant. He wanted me to tell my story. My testimony.

"You're scaring me. What's wrong?" Scharae asked. She'd heard my sniffles and muffled crying. I was unable to speak clearly, so she attempted to calm me down.

"Scharae, God just spoke to me. He told me that I have to tell my story," I managed to get out.

"My God!" Scharae whispered.

For God to reveal such an assignment to me while I was on the phone with Scharae was uncanny. You see, Scharae and I used to go at it a *lot* about this particular subject. She would talk about the importance of me sharing my testimony to help others, and I would always tell her that my testimony was my business, not anyone else's. I'm a private person. I felt like as long as me and my girls were okay, that was all that mattered, and that was all that anyone needed to know.

However, Scharae would explain that I was being selfish by keeping my testimony to myself. She would say, "When God brings you through, your duty is to help someone else! This is how you pay reverence for the grace that He gave you." The mere fact that the Holy Spirit had so clearly revealed Himself to me once again, this time with a witness to it, was of major importance. His words were also confirmation; others, including my former hairstylist, Angel, had told me before that I had books in me.

I told Scharae that I needed to get off the phone and be with the Lord in silence.

"I agree, but before you go, let's pray," she said. Scharae prayed a beautiful prayer, and then we hung up. I continued to drive to work in silence, and in tears, with the Lord.

As I rode along and enjoyed this intimate time with the Lord, He started to order my steps. First, He told me to not have my daily conference calls with Mia and Scharae for the next seven days. I was supposed to be in deep worship and meditation with Him only – no distractions. After work, I called both Mia and Scharae and notified them that for the next seven days, I would not be having morning conferences with them. I could speak with them, just not at our regular time in the morning. Both of my sisters were encouraging and understanding.

Next, God revealed to me how I was supposed to tell my story. I knew that He'd clearly told me to tell my story, but the details about how I was to tell it were missing. I asked Him for insight. *God, what do you mean, "Tell my story?" You want me to get up in front of the congregation and spill my guts? Is that the platform, Lord?* During the seven days of morning solitude and meditation, God revealed this detail of His plan to me. It was so crystal clear that I could not believe it: He told me to write a book. *A book! God, I am not a writer,* I thought. I was scared, not only about writing but about what I was to write – my testimony. However, out of obedience to God, I moved forward. I would complete this project that God Himself had assigned to me.

The Holy Spirit showed me visions and glimpses into God's plan for my life. It was so amazing! It was so huge, I couldn't imagine ever being able to dream something so big by myself. By the seventh day of my intimate time with the Lord, I not only had my title of my book, which is "Hide and Seek," but I also had my chapter titles in sequential order. I thought, *My God, You are mighty!*

The number seven symbolizes completion. On the eighth day, I was able to tell only a chosen few people about me writing a book. This book was to be a movement, and the Holy Spirit showed me who was to be a part of the movement: the beautiful women who had been a sign of God's movement in my life. They had spiritually supported me as I had moved through the process of God removing so many things from my life, including all of the ugliness, pain, heartbreak, brokenness, lies, deceit, selfishness, immaturity... the list could go on and on. He makes all things new, and He made me brand new, too. These ladies would represent my support system throughout the book project when I would cry, "I can't do this! It's too much!"

So began my journey to try to do something that I did not know was already in me. *I'm too broken to write a book,* I thought. *I like to be low-key and fly under the radar. That's my comfortable place*, I began with my excuses.

I was also concerned about what others would say when they read the truth of my testimony. *God wants me to write a tell-all book exposing myself and my girls to strangers' opinions,* I thought. This thought evoked a sense of fear in me. However, it was what the enemy would have me to believe in order to scare me away from completing the project. The truth was that God had called me to write the book, so He was going to cover me. I was His child, so I knew that I had been delivered, favored and protected. Thus, it was my duty and honor to have been tasked with this challenge. There was nothing to fear.

Philippians 4:13, a Bible verse which says, "I can do all things through Christ Jesus who strengthens me," became my weapon against the enemy. I spoke it aloud to remind myself of it whenever the enemy attempted to attack or minimize me, trying to convince me that I couldn't complete the task or discourage me from doing so.

I began to prepare my mind and my spirit to start the writing process. All of my sisters were supportive: Scharae, Michelle, Mia, Tiffany, Charlie, Tiny, Roxy and Angel. Other than sharing the project with these ladies, God told me to keep quiet; no one else needed to know... *especially* Justin. If Justin had heard about what I was doing, my life would have been in constant turmoil.

Before I wrote a word, I consulted with Sierra. She and I had had an opportunity to talk in person when she came home for her summer break. After I told her about what God had instructed me to do, Sierra was in full support. She expressed that she was proud of me for being transparent about my story, and she assured me that I had her blessing. This warmed my heart.

When God gives you an assignment or orders you to do something, He will work everything out, and He will provide everything that is needed for you to execute the assignment. This does not mean the enemy will not attack while you are trying to fulfill what God has told you to do; in fact, you can expect him to attack even more. He knows that God has something great in store for you as you walk in obedience to what God has spoken, and he will do all he can to stop it.

However, although the enemy attacks and attacks so that you can get distracted from your assignment, react to his schemes, and get tired, don't let anything stop you from reaching God's plans for you. As long as you stay focused on your assignment, the Lord's plan shall prevail. I am a witness!

Throughout the course of writing this book, the enemy used Justin incessantly. Whether or not Justin knew that he was being used as the devil's puppet in my life during this time, I don't know. What I do know is that just as I had gone to a new level through the process of working, living, parenting, and beginning to write this book, Justin was following me and harassing me every step of the way. Our divorce filing was still moving forward, and just like God had promised, I didn't have to do anything, including pay one red cent to end my marriage. However, Justin's behavior during the time that I was writing my testimony was highly unsettling, and I was very stressed and anxious.

One day at work, I felt exhausted and stressed. I wasn't feeling well and I needed to go home, but I knew I couldn't drive in this condition. I called my nephew to see if he could pick me up. There was no answer. Next, I called Scharae, who worked right up the street from my office. No answer. Eventually, as my symptoms increased, I reluctantly called Justin. I was desperate because I felt I had no other choice, and I was hoping that he would be compassionate enough to come and pick me up, considering the circumstances. I justified calling him by saying to myself, *He's Kennedy's father, and he knows how to take care of me when I'm ill.* I tried calling him about 10 times, but there was no answer. Then, I called Scharae again. This time, she answered.

"Hey, Sister," she said.

"Hey. I don't feel good," I moaned.

"What's wrong?" she asked.

"I feel weak," I said.

With my phone in my hand and Scharae still on the other end, I stood up to get my manager's attention. My heart was racing, and I felt dizzy. I can remember taking a couple of steps towards my manager, and then I fainted – right in the middle of my office floor.

I could hear the commotion of my co-workers, and I could also hear Scharae as she began to yell into the phone, hoping that someone could hear her voice. She was already en route to my office. A co-worker overheard her yelling and picked my phone up. Scharae told my co-worker that she was already downstairs and asked to see me.

When I woke up, I was in Scharae's arms. Someone from my office had called the paramedics, but I did not want to get into the ambulance or be taken to the hospital; I just wanted to get to Kennedy ASAP. Scharae had already called one of our girlfriends to pick Kennedy up from her after-school program.

"She's good," Scharae reassured me. "Now, let me take you to the doctor."

"I just want to see Kennedy," I repeated.

"Right now, you need to go and have your vitals checked," she insisted. "You need to find out why you fainted."

Scharae and I made our way to her car. As we were driving, I started to feel light-headed again. I also started to hyperventilate. Scharae wanted to help me, but I was being stubborn. I kept insisting that I just wanted to see Kennedy.

My phone rang. It was Justin. I told him what had happened, and he asked about Kennedy. I assured him that she was okay and that my girlfriend was picking her up from her after-school program.

"Tell Scharae to bring you to my place," he said. "Since your car is still at your office, we need to go get it."

"You brought up a good point," I said.

Justin advised that Scharae and I should pick him up, and then we would go get my car together. Then, Justin and I would get in my car, and he would take me to Urgent Care. We would send Scharae to go pick up Kennedy from our girlfriend's place. When Justin and I were done at the hospital, we would pick up Kennedy from Scharae's place.

At the time, it sounded like a good plan. Scharae picked up Justin, then dropped Justin and me off at my car. Then, she headed to pick up Kennedy. Justin told Scharae that he would call her and keep her posted. Then, Justin and I headed to the Urgent Care center together.

The entire time we were at Urgent Care, Justin was gentle and attentive to me. He filled in all of my medical paperwork and even accompanied me to the exam room when I was called to the back. He stayed in the room as the doctors began trying to figure out why I'd fainted.

Probably a good hour after I'd been in the hospital bed, Justin jumped up and said he was hungry.

"I'll be right back," he said. "I'm going to grab something to eat real quick. Did you want anything?"

"No," I said. I was still feeling loopy. Off he went in my car to pick up something to eat.

By the time Justin returned, I was talking with the doctor. My tests had come back, and there was nothing alarming in the results.

The doctor asked if I had been under any stress lately. I responded, "Yes. I am currently going through a divorce."

She told me to take it easy, advised me to take the next day off from work, and instructed me to get a lot of rest. I agreed. The doctors released me from Urgent Care, and then Justin and I headed to pick up Kennedy from Scharae's house.

On the way to Scharae's, Justin made a suggestion. He thought it would be a good idea for him to stay over – for Kennedy's sake.

I thought about it. *What if I had another fainting spell and Kennedy was there by herself?* I questioned. In light of this consideration, although I *did not* like the plan, I agreed to it. However, I made it clear to Justin up front that he was staying in the living room. *No* funny business. He agreed.

We picked up Kennedy from Scharae's, and the three of us headed to my apartment. *Who would have thought when I woke up this morning that by the end of day, I would have fainted and allowed Justin to stay the night at my house?* I wondered. I shook my head in disbelief at the private conversation I had just had with myself.

When Kennedy got into the car and saw the two of us, she looked completely confused.

"Mom, why is Dad going to our house?" she asked. Kennedy usually never said a word, but I could tell that her high level of confusion had driven her to go ahead and ask about what was happening.

I did not answer Kennedy's question. I simply locked eyes with her and gave her that *Hush, child!* look that told her that this was not the time to be asking any questions. She sat back and quieted herself in the backseat, looking out of the window.

When we arrived at my apartment, Kennedy jumped into the bath and started her routine to get ready for school the next day. Justin made her something to eat for dinner. Although I appreciated his help, from the moment that Justin set foot in my house, I was anxious and uneasy. I held on to this same unsettling feeling all night.

Disregarding the clear parameters that I'd discussed with him before I agreed to let him stay over, Justin tried to make advances towards me in the middle of the night. I couldn't believe that he'd picked such a moment to try and push his own agenda on me. I couldn't take it. I woke Kennedy up and told her to put her jacket and shoes on.

"Why, Mommy?" she asked in a sleepy voice.

"We're taking your father home," I said.

"What?" Justin asked. We were all in my master bedroom, and Kennedy was in my bed; I did not want to be in my room alone that night with Justin in the apartment. Justin had been sitting on the edge of the bed and heard me speaking to Kennedy.

"Yes. Something doesn't feel right. You don't belong here. It's time for you to go," I said.

I was pleasantly surprised that Justin did not fight or argue with me. Instead, he just went into the living room to grab his backpack and jacket.

"Okay," he said, with a sneaky smirk on his face. I would find out a couple of months later why he did not resist.

I dropped Justin off at his parents' house, and Kennedy and I went back home.

The next morning, Scharae and Mia called to check on me. I told them what had happened and how in the middle of the night, I took Justin home.

Mia said, "I thought the idea of him spending the night was *crazy*!"

"It was," I told her, "but I didn't want to freak Kennedy out if I happened to faint again. I would rather be uncomfortable than have Kennedy scared and alone." I could tell that my sister did not agree with my decision to initially allow Justin to stay over, but she understood where I was coming from regarding Kennedy.

After that situation, I knew in my heart that I could not see myself reconciling with Justin. I was a different woman now, transformed by God's love. The insecurities that had plagued me in the past no longer existed. I had truly experienced real love from God, and it had *changed* me.

Three Sundays after my fainting spell, I attended church and sat next to Tiny like I usually did. However, this Sunday was different. Although my bishop normally preached on Sundays, there was a guest speaker on this particular day. My bishop was there, but he'd yielded his pulpit to an attending pastor, who happened to be female, to deliver the Sunday morning message. She spoke about relationships, new and old. During the course of her message, she made a powerful statement that resonated deeply within my soul and spirit. She said, "You are free to love again."

The pastor's words hit me to my core, so much so that as she was still talking, I went to the altar and planted a seed of offering in agreement with her words. I was hopeful that one day, I, too, would enter into a relationship the right way: I would meet a man, and then I would take this prospect to God first, seeking His permission to move forward with a relationship.

Right after church, I was standing next to Tiny, who was talking to a very handsome gentleman. She talked to me to get my attention.

"Anthony, this is my sister, Bree," she said. We all called one another "sister" as a term of endearment.

He smiled and shook my hand.

"Nice to meet you," I said as I smiled back.

"Likewise," he said.

The dude was *fine*! I remember seeing him on the church campus about six months prior. I would always do a double-take, because he could wear a suit *right*. I'd assumed that he'd had a girl or someone special in his life. I'd never noticed him double taking on me.

"Nice to put a name with the suit," I said, subtly suggesting that I had seen and admired his style of dress from a distance in the past.

After our introduction, Tiny and Anthony walked away together. It was raining that day, and Tiny did not have her umbrella, so the gentleman said that he would accompany Tiny to her car using his umbrella. I said goodbye to them and headed to the Youth Department to find Scharae in children's church.

Scharae was in children's church picking up Christian and Kennedy. We both sat down for a few minutes, discussing how powerful the sermon had been. All of a sudden, Tiny came walking into the room.

"Sister, I thought you left!" I said.

Tiny smiled and waved a card that she held in her hand.

"Bree, do you remember my friend Anthony that I just introduced you to?" she asked.

"Yes," I said, confused. "What's up?"

"Well, he said that you're beautiful, and he wanted me to give you his card!"

"*Really?*" I asked with a smile.

"Yes, Girl!" she beamed. Tiny continued, "Now, you already know that I am too much! I told him my sister has been through a lot, and she does not need no shenanigans in her life. So, if you had some slick reason to talk to her, you can go ahead and keep your contact information. He said, 'No! No shenanigans here!' So, here you go, Sister!" She handed the business card over to me, and I gladly accepted it.

"What's his deal?" I asked, curious.

"Honestly," Tiny began, "Anthony is a great guy! He's focused, has goals and priorities, and above all, he loves the Lord. If there's nothing else between you guys, I believe the Lord is showing you that you can attract a man of his caliber in order to help you through your season. You are worthy, whether you just end up having a friendly conversation, a friendship, or more. He's a good man."

I began to have intentional interactions with Anthony when I saw him. I had to admit that I enjoyed our conversations and innocent visit at church. He was aware that I was in process of a divorce, and he was respectful of the fact that technically, I was another man's wife until my divorce was finalized.

All my sisters loved Anthony. Not long after he and I had begun having conversations, Mia had planned to come to town for a few days to visit her family; I was excited for her to meet Anthony, too.

Whenever Mia came to town, she would typically stay with me, and we would have a great time. However, Mia had no tolerance for Justin's obsessive antics. Whenever she was in town and he would start to obsessively call my phone, she would answer it, and then they would both go off on each other. It was *very* explosive! She could not stand his bully tactics with me, and neither she nor Scharae appreciated the anxiety that his behavior brought into my life. Scharae was no angel with Justin, either; they'd had their own history of yelling matches about his obsessive calling and his stalking behavior.

This visit for Mia would be different; she was finally going to meet a man in my life who was making me happy rather than causing me constant grief.

Mia arrived in town, and as we always do, the three of us hung out together. Since Mia doesn't come to town very often, when she does, Scharae and I usually take a day or two off of work to reconnect over lunches, dinners, and other events. We constantly laugh and enjoy one another's company during these rare times when our trio is reunited.

Mia came to church with me and met Anthony there. She agreed that he was handsome, and she said that he'd seemed very sweet.

"Go slow, Sister," she warned. "Ask *a lot* of freaking questions. Observe him and all of his emotions. Most importantly, pray to the Lord for direction."

"Check, check, and check!" I said confidently. "All of the above is already in motion!"

"Good!" Mia said, smiling. "Because we can't handle another fool!"

"That is NOT an option!" Scharae chimed in.

"Mmm, okay!" I said. I was glad that I had my sisters' support.

November 30th started out as normally as any other day. Justin was aware that Mia was in town, because he'd seen pictures of us together posted on social media. After he saw the pictures, he made his daily phone call to me, requesting to speak to Kennedy. I told him that I was trying to get her to school on time, and having a conversation at the moment would only slow her down. I said that she could talk to him when we were in the car. He said okay.

Mia was in the kitchen making herself a cup of coffee. I was already showered and dressed. I had Scharae on the phone with the speaker on.

"What's the game plan for today?" Mia asked.

My suggestion was that Mia get dressed and leave with Kennedy and me. After I dropped Kennedy off at school, Mia and I would meet up with Scharae.

"Okay," she said. "Let me finish my coffee, and then I'll start to get ready."

"Sister, hurry!" I said. "I don't want Kennedy to be late for school!"

Scharae interrupted, saying, "No, Mia should stay, and you and Kennedy head out. I'm already en route, dropping

Christian off at school. We can get Mia in an hour or two after we run this errand."

Mia seconded Scharae's idea. "I like that plan! I can already feel a spirit of Bree rushing me to get ready, and I have no patience for that nonsense today!" she said sarcastically.

"Whatever, fool!" I said. I grabbed my keys and separated my car key from my house key. "Here. Just in case you go outside, you can lock the door. Okay?"

"Thanks," Mia said. "Just put it on the coffee table."

"We are about to go, so say bye to your auntie, Ken," I said to Kennedy as we headed for the door.

"Bye, Auntie!" Kennedy shouted. Mia said goodbye back to her.

"Mia, lock this door!" I called back to her.

"I'm right behind you, 'cause I'm about to jump in the shower," she said. Kennedy and I headed out the door and to our car.

As we drove toward the freeway, my phone began to blow up again. I didn't answer it right away; I was having a brief chat with Anthony. After the 17th freaking call, I just handed the phone to Kennedy as it rang.

"Hi, Daddy! Good morning. Yes, we left. Yes, we're on the freeway now. Ummm... we are by..." Kennedy ducked her head to confirm the street names on the freeway sign.

Kennedy had the same strange conversation with her father every morning. I'd just thought that Justin had always run out of topics to talk about, so he would ask random questions about our location just to keep the conversation flowing. I had no idea that I was going to soon find out why they had these conversations daily.

"Mommy, Daddy wants to talk to you," she said, stretching out her arm to hand the phone to me.

Irritated, I rolled my eyes and took the phone from Kennedy.

"Hello? What's up?"

"Dang! You can't answer your phone?" he asked.

"I was busy," I replied.

"Yeah, busy alright," he said.

"What's up?" I asked hurriedly.

"Nothing. So, you going to work today?" Before I could answer, he sarcastically replied for me. "Naw, I guess not. You and your crew hanging out again, right?" There was complete silence on my end. "Oh, am I *bothering* you?"

I violently shook my head up and down, still not saying a word.

"Okay," he said. "Going to let you go. Bye." I hung the phone up.

Exactly 10 minutes after that phone call, I received another one. This time it was from Mia.

"Hey, Girly," I calmly answered.

"Bree!" she said frantically.

"What?" Her voice had caused me to become instantly nervous. "Are you okay?"

"NO!" she yelled.

"What happened? What's wrong, girl?" I asked.

"Justin is here!"

"You mean outside my house? You just saw him?"

"No, *in* your damn house!" she shrieked.

"WHAT! What do you mean *in* my house? I *told* your ass to lock the door when we were leaving!"

Mia's next words sent me into a panic. "I did! He has a *key!*"

"What the hell are you talking about? A *key*? Mia, you're tripping! Did you see him outside my house and think he has a key?"

"No!" she yelled. "This ninja was actually IN your damn apartment!"

I had completely forgotten that Kennedy was still in the car. I was severely cursing and crying all at the same time, and this had caused her to begin to cry. As Mia and I were talking, Justin was also calling; he'd already called at least 20 times since she and I had been on the phone. I did not acknowledge his calls.

I needed to immediately get a grip. My baby was scared, Mia was sick, and my nerves were shot. I exited the freeway and turned onto the street that led to Kennedy's school.

"Mommy, why did my daddy do that?" Kennedy had heard everything because the car had Bluetooth speakers.

"I don't know, Baby. Listen, Mommy will pick you up a little early today. Don't worry. Everything will be okay," I said, trying to comfort her.

"Mommy, maybe my daddy did it on accident," she said in her little voice in defense of her father. At the moment, I didn't have words adequate enough to help her understand that this had not been an accident at all. This baby adored her dad, and my heart broke for her at that moment.

"Mommy is going to find out, okay?" She nodded and gave me a big hug and kiss. Tears fell from my eyes. *She is so innocent and loving*, I thought to myself.

As soon as I saw Kennedy walk into her classroom, I frantically called Scharae on her mobile phone. I had already planned to meet up and run errands with her after dropping Kennedy off, but this couldn't wait until I saw her. I had to tell her now!

"Hello?" she answered.

"OMG! This ninja broke into my *house*!" I shrieked.

"Bree, what are you talking about?" she asked.

"Justin came into my *house*!" I repeated.

"He lost his good mind, now!" Scharae said, shocked at Justin's audacity. I told her that I was on my way and that we would continue the conversation when I picked her up at our church; this was our designated meeting point.

Once I pulled up to the church, Scharae jumped into my car. My phone was still blowing up because Justin kept calling me, but I did not answer. We called Mia back. She answered on the first ring and began to tell us what had happened.

"When you guys left," she started, "I locked the door. I finished my coffee and got my clothes together to take a shower. After I took a shower, I decided to only put on my t-shirt and panties. I was sitting in the living room. I heard someone skipping up the stairs, but I thought it was one of your neighbors. Then, I heard someone fumbling with keys. They put the freaking key in your door! I turned to look at the coffee table and saw that the key you'd left me was still there, so I turned down the TV a bit lower to listen. When I saw the lock turn, I was shocked! When the door opened, there he was: Justin walked in! That's when he realized that he wasn't alone in the apartment. He *saw* me staring at him! He said, "Oh, *shit*!" Then, he closed and locked the door, and he quickly ran down the stairs! I ran into your room to see if I could catch him leaving. The fool was parked in your carport!"

Both Scharae's and my mouth were wide open. We were speechless. I couldn't believe Justin had a key to my place! I was so mad, I started to drive like I was about to Ghost Ride the Whip, moving about from lane to lane fast and recklessly!

See this, Scharae called out, “Pull this car over now!” so I did. With the emotional condition that I was in, it was safer that she drive anyway.

“Y’all need to hurry back,” Mia said. “I don't know if this fool is coming back.”

“We are on our way, Dawg,” Scharae said.

My phone beeped again. Before I looked down at it, I thought, *Mia, we said that we’re on our way!* As soon as I looked down at the phone screen, however, I saw that it was the psychopath. *Let me see what he’s saying*, I thought. I took a deep breath to control my anger before I answered.

“Hello?”

“What’s up?” he asked. “Did Kennedy make it to school okay?”

“Why wouldn’t she?” I questioned.

In my mind, I was thinking, *This fool wants me to play along with the crazy conversation. Dude you have to know that by now I’m aware of what you did!*

In my anger and frustration, I just blurted out, “Justin, I am not going to sit here and continue to play these games with you! Why the hell do you have a key to my spot?”

“Huh?” He responded as if he had no idea of what I was talking about. That was when I *lost* it!

“You just walked in on Mia! She saw you with her own eyes! Dude, you have a key to my apartment. She has a description of what you’re wearing from head to toe, not to mention the make, model and color of the car you’re driving!”

“That was not me. I’m clear across town,” he said, pretending.

“Save that crap!” I yelled.

“Bree, that wasn’t me,” he insisted.

“You’re a liar! She saw you and heard you trot up the stairs before you entered my apartment. What a freaking violation! Wait a minute. How did you get keys to my apartment?" I asked, perplexed.

There was silence. My mind was racing a mile a minute trying to figure out how, where, and when he could have possibly gotten a key to my place. Then, it hit me.

"Oh, my GOD! The *only* time you had access to me and my keys was two months ago, when I fainted at work!" My heart was beating fast and my head was pounding. "How *could* you? I remember now. You asked to borrow my car to get something to eat. While I laid in a hospital bed waiting for my test results, Dude, you made copies of my *key*? That's it! That is the only time since our separation that I allowed you to be close. You did this to me in my most vulnerable state? Really? Who *does* that? Why do you keep violating me? This is all making sense to me now!" I ranted.

I took a breath and continued, "*That's* why you accuse me of shopping so much! *That's* how you know when I'm on my cycle! You've been in my house, going through my belongings, you *freak*! Now that I think of it, a few weeks ago when I came home from work, my walk-in closet light was left on. I *never* leave anything on. I double check everything before I leave. Even Kennedy thought it was strange. It was *you*!"

I never gave Justin an opportunity to talk, agree or make a rebuttal. Everything made sense now.

I wasn't finished. "You always question Kennedy when you talk to her on the phone about where are we, what street, are we on the freeway... you've been sizing up if you should go to my place! I *hate* you!" I screamed.

As many problems as we'd had over the years, I had never used the words "I hate you" with him. That morning, in the car, for the first time ever, I cussed Justin out in such a way that he knew I was done for good!

I took three deep breaths to slow down my speech and heart rate. I wanted him to hear every word that was going to come out of my mouth.

I very calmly said, “Sir, I am calling the cops. You will have a restraining order on your ass before the week is up.” I hung up the phone.

Scharae and I stopped by my apartment to pick Mia up, and then we headed to the courthouse to file the restraining order. On the way to the courthouse, I called Justin’s true blue friends and told them what had happened. I shared what my plans were regarding the restraining order. They were shocked and disappointed, but they understood that I was doing what was best for me and my daughters.

By the end of day, God and the judge granted me an emergency restraining order. We were due in court on the 21st of December. That date is so significant to me. You see, two years prior, on that very date, was when I’d finally told Mia and Scharae the truth about Justin. That was the very day that he and I had separated. Now, two years later, on the same date, I was going to go to court regarding this incident. I had been stalked by Justin for two years with phone calls, drive-bys, and pop-ups. God said, “It all stops today!”

Please understand that this whole situation had not been a coincidence; it was God revealing Justin’s secret actions to me so I could do what I needed to do, once and for all. Mia was *supposed* to be in town, and Justin was *supposed* to walk in on her. God’s grace and protection is sufficient and real.

My locks were changed that same day, the restraining order was now in place, and just as I warned Justin, he was served with the restraining order at the end of the week. God did not stop there, though. Exactly seven days from the day

Justin walked into my house, my finalized divorce papers were mailed to me! I am now officially divorced and have a temporary restraining order against Justin.

The kicker for me is this very book, which I had been writing throughout this whole process. Although it was still under wraps, never did I leave my book at home; I always kept it with me so I could write in it whenever the feeling hit me. God had assigned me to write this book, so the book was always covered and protected! Isn't God *amazing*? I truly believe that if Justin had any notion that I was writing about my story, he would have probably destroyed it. By God's grace, the opportunity was never made available to him. God's will shall be done!

On December 20th, Scharae and I were back at the airport picking up Mia; she was *not* going to miss the opportunity to show up in court, along with Scharae, on December 21st to support me.

The morning of my court hearing, Scharae, Mia and I got ready to go. My heart was filled with anxiousness. For the past month, I had not heard from Justin at all; the restraining order that I had against him stipulated that he could not have any contact with me. It was kind of strange not to have my phone vibrate every five minutes, but the peace that I now had was calming.

The three of us made it to the courtroom and sat down. A few moments later, Justin appeared. The look on his face when he saw us was classic. The three of us started to giggle quietly to ourselves; we especially knew that he was going to make that look when he saw Mia.

We were there for half the day before the clerk called our case. When it was our turn on the docket, the judge read my incident report aloud and asked the respondent, Justin, if what I had written on the report was true.

Justin bravely responded, “Yes, Your Honor. It’s all true. I did what Bree wrote. If I may, Your Honor, I would like to take this time to apologize to her personally and to her sisters as well, Mia and Scharae. I would also like to thank you both for standing by her. I did a lot of wrongs things to her, and for that, I lost my marriage and family. I was spinning out of control, and now, I understand that I need to leave her alone.”

The court was silent. I was in tears and Scharae was, too. I think that for the first time, she could see that he was not well. The judge thanked Justin for his honesty and agreed that I need to have some distance from him. He extended the temporary restraining order for three years.

God’s will was done. Everything that was ugly, broken and evil in my life, God had turned into something beautiful. Ashes are a sign of cleansing; from them, God makes all things new.

In 2015, God very clearly spoke to me, giving me an assignment: to write this book and to expose the enemy and his tricks in order to help others. However, God does not only talk to me; He is always talking to us – to *you*. Are you listening?

When God gave me this assignment, He did not give it to me for the purpose of creating a platform to tear down Justin; that’s not the intent of my story at all. On the contrary, I pray for Justin daily and pray for God’s best in his life. After all, we still have an amazing daughter that we have to raise, and I want her father to be all that he can be in God so that our daughter can become all she can become. Instead, the intent of my story is to help you to understand how to respond to the warning signs, the red flags, and the writing on the wall that

God shows us in life; warning signs, red flags and writings on the wall that we often choose to ignore in order to do things our way instead of His.

God shows us these warning signs, red flags, and writings on the wall in life because He loves us and only wants the best for us. Therefore, when He speaks, listen. When He shows you something is off, don't look the other way, pay attention. When He taps you on the shoulder, don't ignore Him or tell Him that you're too busy for Him, give Him your full attention.

When we do things our own way and according to our own wisdom, we are prone to produce outcomes that lead to secrets, shame, isolation, embarrassment, and destruction – lives worth hiding. However, when we seek Him, His way, and His wisdom, He can reveal His plan for our lives and give us clear instructions about the assignment that He has for us.

When you do seek Him, though, don't be surprised if He tells you to take the things you've been keeping under wraps for years and share them with the world! These might be the very things that He will use to bring healing and deliverance to others, for His glory. Thus, I ask you. What are *you* hiding?